Name ____________________ Date ____________

Reading and Writing Numbers

Circle groups of ten.
Write the number.
Draw a line to the correct number word.

1. 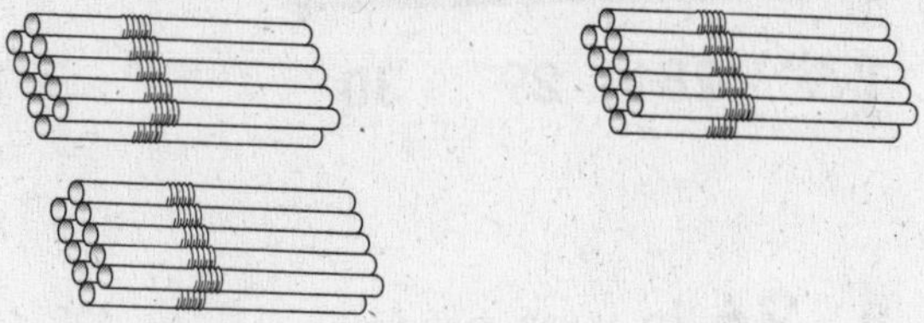 30

2. 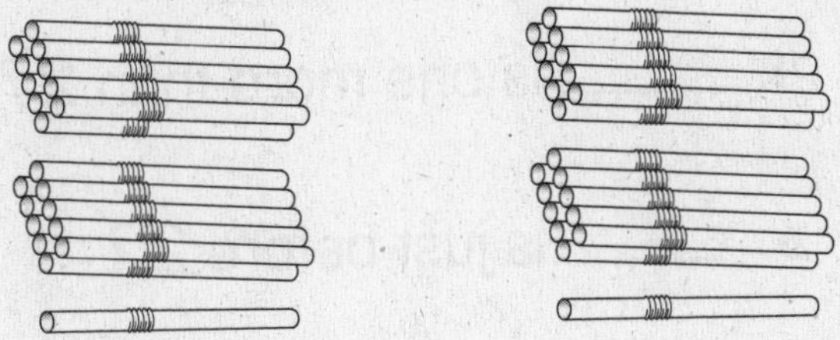 ______

3. 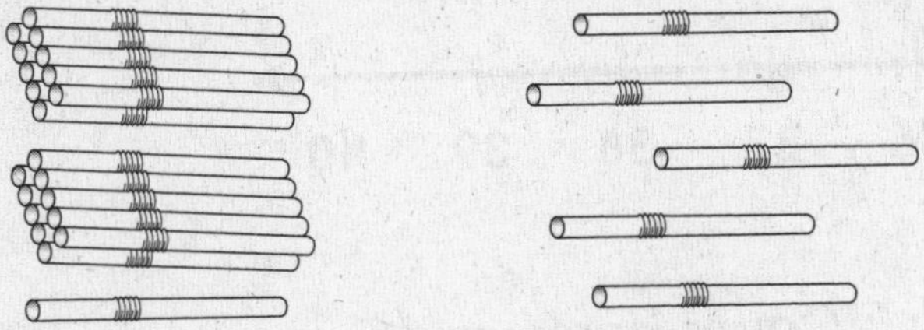 ______

4. 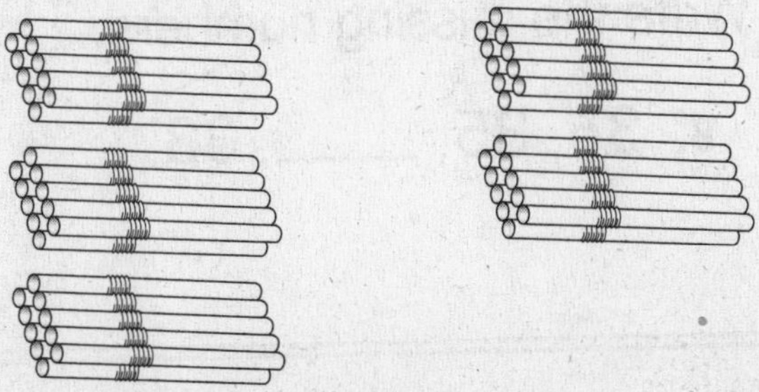 ______

twenty-six

fifty

thirty

forty-two

Test Prep

Fill in the ○ for the correct answer. NH means Not Here.

5. How many straws are there?

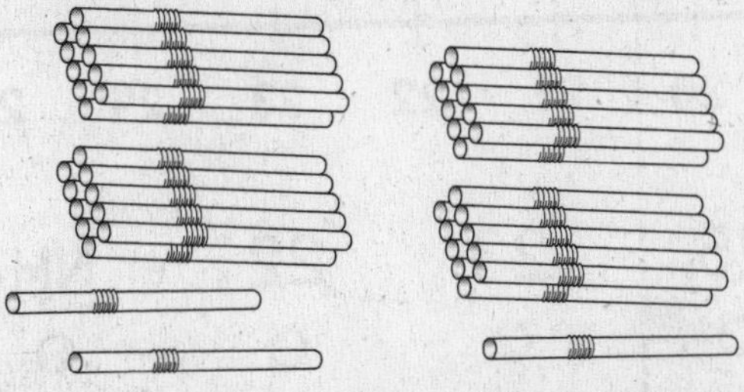

45	43	34	NH
○	○	○	○

Use with text pages 7–9.

Name ______________________ Date ______________

Practice 1.2

Ordering Numbers

Use the number line below.
Complete the sentence.

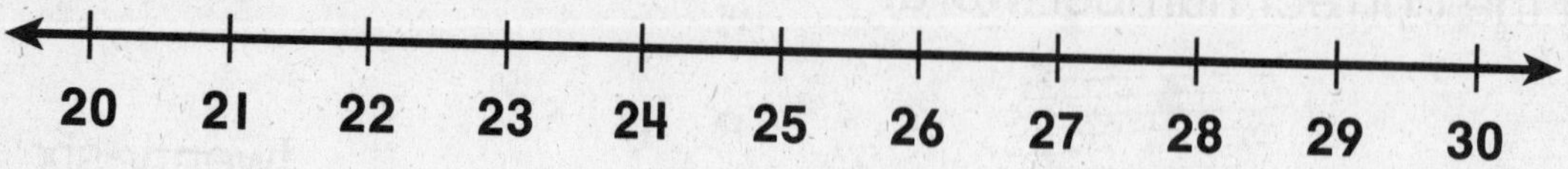

1. 24 is just before 25
2. 26 is just after ______
3. 29 is one less than ______
4. ______ is one more than 27
5. 23 is just after ______
6. ______ is just before 22

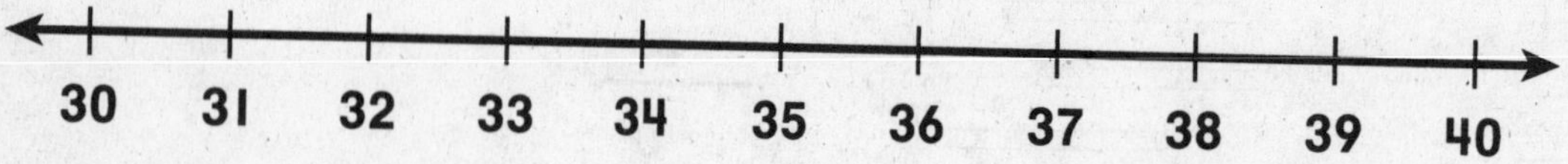

Count forward.
Write the missing numbers.

7. 33, 34, ______, ______, 37

Count backward.
Write the missing numbers.

8. 36, 35, ______, 33, ______

Test Prep

Fill in the ○ for the correct answer. NH means Not Here.

9. Which number comes just after 21?

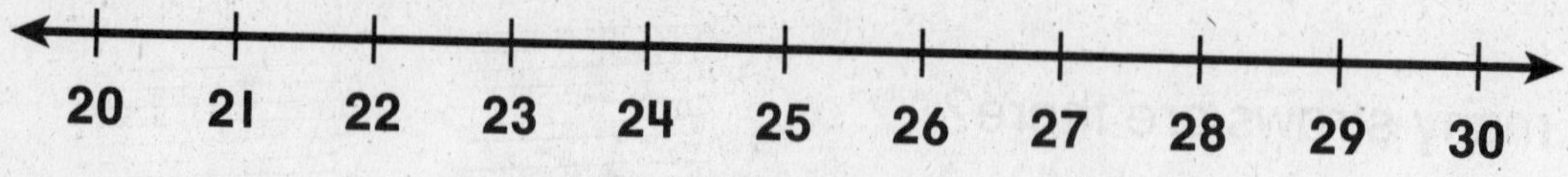

25	23	22	NH
○	○	○	○

Use with text pages 11–12.

Name ____________________ Date ____________

Comparing Numbers

Write how many there are.
Circle the greater number.
Write **more** or **fewer**.

1. 

5

7

There are fewer  than .

2. 

____

____

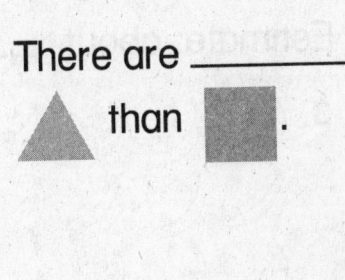

There are ____  than .

Write > or <.

3. 36 ◯ 25
4. 45 ◯ 49
5. 12 ◯ 11
6. 24 ◯ 29
7. 19 ◯ 15
8. 42 ◯ 44
9. 33 ◯ 27
10. 50 ◯ 47
11. 16 ◯ 23

Test Prep

Fill in the ○ for the correct answer. NH means Not Here.

12. Which number sentence is true?

42 > 52	31 > 25	19 > 31	NH
○	○	○	○

Use with text pages 13–14.

Name ______________________ Date ____________

Practice 1.4

Estimating How Many

Estimate how many.

You can circle a group of ten to help you. Think about how many tens in all.

1. 

Estimate: about 30

2. 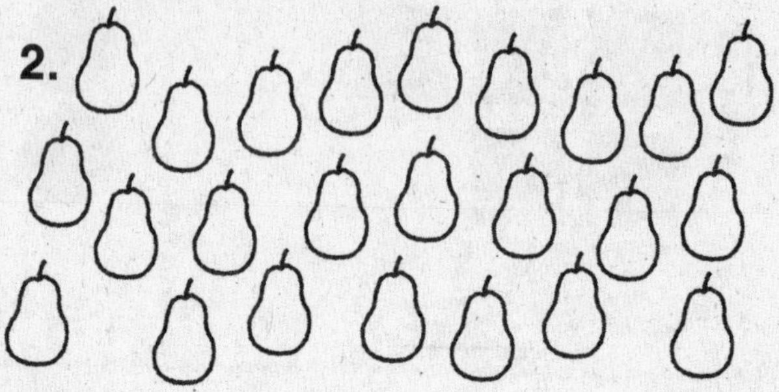

Estimate: about ____________

3. 

Estimate: about ____________

4. 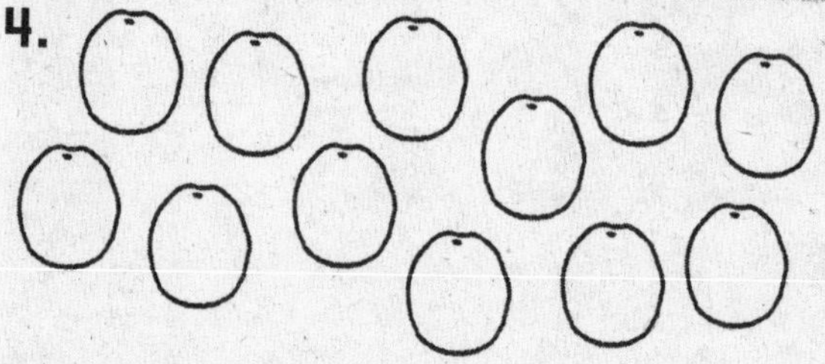

Estimate: about ____________

5. About how many are there? Circle the best estimate.

about 30 about 50 about 70

Test Prep

Fill in the ○ for the correct answer. NH means Not Here.

6. Estimate how many.

10	20	30	NH
○	○	○	○

Explain how you chose your estimate.

Use with text pages 17–18.

Name ______________________ Date ______________

Reasonable Answers

Circle the most reasonable answer.

1. There are 8 girls playing soccer. Then 2 leave to go home. Are there more girls or fewer girls playing soccer?	6 girls more girls fewer girls
2. Olivia plays hoop ball. She has 5 balls to throw in a hoop. She gets the first 3 in the hoop. How many throws does she have left?	none 2 throws 3 throws
3. There are 5 children in the park. Then 4 other children come to play. Are there more children or fewer children playing?	10 children more children fewer children

Test Prep

Fill in the ○ for the correct answer. NH means Not Here.

4. Ruby strings 4 beads. Jake strings 3 beads.
Does Ruby string more beads or fewer beads than Jake?

7 beads	more beads	fewer beads	NH
○	○	○	○

Use with text pages 19–20.

Name ____________________ Date ____________

Practice 2.1

Addition Properties

Add.

1.
```
  5     3
+ 3   + 5
---   ---
  8     8
```
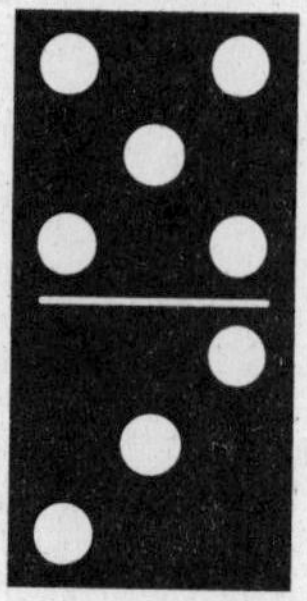

2.
```
  0     4
+ 4   + 0
---   ---
```

3.
```
  7     2
+ 2   + 7
---   ---
```

4.
```
  3     1
+ 1   + 3
---   ---
```

5.
```
  8     0
+ 0   + 8
---   ---
```

6.
```
  0
+ 5
---
```

7.
```
  1
+ 5
---
```

8.
```
  6
+ 3
---
```

9.
```
  4
+ 2
---
```

10.
```
  1
+ 7
---
```

11.
```
  7
+ 0
---
```

12. 8 + 1 = ____

13. 8 + 2 = ____

14. 0 + 6 = ____

Test Prep

Fill in the ○ for the correct answer. NH means Not Here.

15. 6 + 4 = ____ + 6

4	6	10	NH
○	○	○	○

Use with text pages 27–28.

Name ____________________ Date ____________

Subtract All or None

$5 - 0 = 5$

$5 - 5 = 0$

Subtract.

1. $\begin{array}{r}6\\-6\\\hline 0\end{array}$	**2.** $\begin{array}{r}2\\-0\\\hline\end{array}$	**3.** $\begin{array}{r}10\\-0\\\hline\end{array}$	**4.** $\begin{array}{r}8\\-8\\\hline\end{array}$
5. $\begin{array}{r}4\\-4\\\hline\end{array}$	**6.** $\begin{array}{r}8\\-8\\\hline\end{array}$	**7.** $\begin{array}{r}1\\-0\\\hline\end{array}$	**8.** $\begin{array}{r}9\\-0\\\hline\end{array}$
9. $\begin{array}{r}1\\-1\\\hline\end{array}$	**10.** $\begin{array}{r}9\\-9\\\hline\end{array}$	**11.** $\begin{array}{r}7\\-0\\\hline\end{array}$	**12.** $\begin{array}{r}1\\-0\\\hline\end{array}$

Test Prep

Fill in the ○ for the correct answer. NH means Not Here.

13. Subtract.

$\begin{array}{r}2\\-\ 0\\\hline\end{array}$

2	20	0	NH
○	○	○	○

Use with text pages 51–52.

Name ______________________ Date ____________

Count Back to Subtract

Use the number line.
Count back to subtract.

Remember
You can use a number line to help you count back.

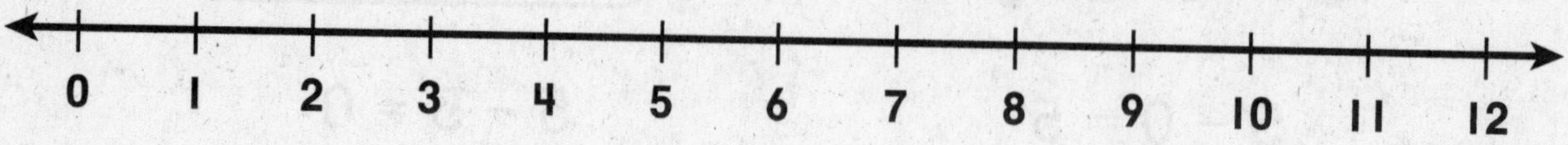

1. 9 − 2 = 7
2. 11 − 1 = ____
3. 10 − 3 = ____
4. 8 − 3 = ____
5. 9 − 3 = ____
6. 6 − 2 = ____
7. 10 − 1 = ____
8. 11 − 3 = ____
9. 5 − 3 = ____

10. 10 − 2	11. 7 − 3	12. 4 − 1	13. 6 − 3
14. 8 − 1	15. 5 − 3	16. 9 − 1	17. 5 − 1

Test Prep

Fill in the ○ for the correct answer. NH means Not Here.

18. Subtract.

12 − 3 = ____

11	10	9	NH
○	○	○	○

Use with text pages 53–54.

Name ______________________ Date ____________

Practice 3.3

Subtract to Compare

Use cubes.
Complete the number sentence.

1. 5 (shaded cubes)
   8 (white cubes)

   How many fewer (shaded cubes) are there?

   8 – ____ = ____

2. 7 (white cubes)
   5 (shaded cubes)

   How many more (white cubes) are there?

   ____ – ____ = ____

3. 9 (shaded cubes)
   3 (white cubes)

   How many more (shaded cubes) are there?

   ____ – ____ = ____

4. 6 (white cubes)
   11 (shaded cubes)

   How many fewer (white cubes) are there?

   ____ – ____ = ____

5. 5 (white cubes)
   13 (shaded cubes)

   How many fewer (white cubes) are there?

   ____ – ____ = ____

6. 15 (shaded cubes)
   7 (white cubes)

   How many more (shaded cubes) are there?

   ____ – ____ = ____

Test Prep

Fill in the ○ for the correct answer. NH means Not Here.

7. Solve.

   6 (shaded cubes)
   9 (white cubes)

   How many fewer (shaded cubes) are there?

2	3	6	NH
○	○	○	○

   Explain how you got your answer by writing the number sentence you used.

   ____

   ____

Use with text pages 55–56.

Name ______________________ Date ____________

Practice 3.4

Use Addition to Subtract

Add or subtract.

Remember
Related facts use the same three numbers.

1. 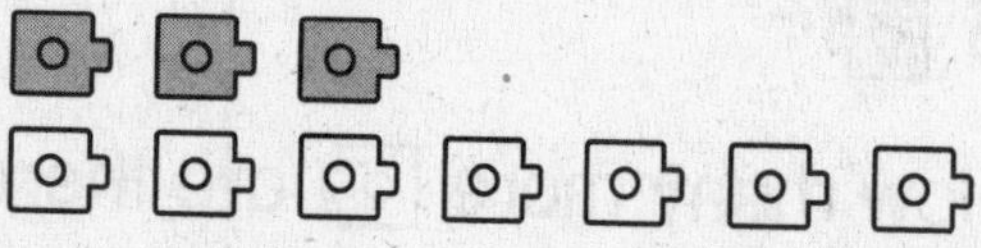

3 + 7 = 10

___ − 7 = 3

2. 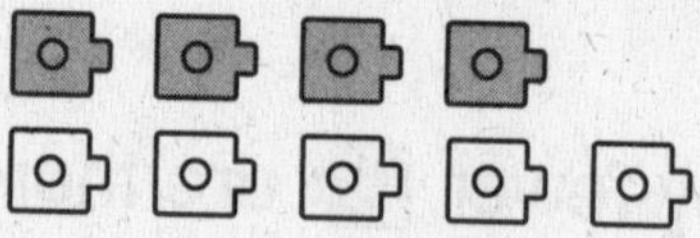

4 + 5 = ___

___ − 5 = ___

3. 7 + 7 = ___
14 − 7 = ___

4. 6 + 9 = ___
15 − 9 = ___

5. 7 + 3 = ___
10 − 3 = ___

6. 2 + 8 = ___
10 − ___ = 2

7. 5 + 4 = ___
___ − 4 = 5

8. 7 + 9 = ___
16 − 9 = ___

9. 3 + 3 = ___
___ − 3 = 3

10. 8 + 7 = ___
15 − ___ = 8

11. 6 + 7 = ___
13 − ___ = 7

Test Prep

Fill in the ○ for the correct answer. NH means Not Here.

12. 5 + 9 = 14

14 − 9 = ___

14	9	5	NH
○	○	○	○

Name ______________________ Date ______________

Practice 3.7

Variables

Find the missing number.

> **Remember**
> A fact family has the same two parts and the same whole.

1. __?__ + 7 = 16
   16 − 7 = ___

2. 15 − __?__ = 8
   15 − 8 = ___

3. 6 + __?__ = 10
   10 − 6 = ___

4. 6 + __?__ = 13
   13 − 6 = ___

5. __?__ + 4 = 9
   9 − 4 = ___

6. 8 + __?__ = 17
   17 − 8 = ___

7. 8 + __?__ = 16
   16 − 8 = ___

8. __?__ + 8 = 15
   15 − 8 = ___

9. 3 + __?__ = 12
   12 − 3 = ___

10. 6 + □ = 10
    10 − 6 = ___

11. □ + 5 = 11
    11 − 5 = ___

12. □ + 4 = 9
    9 − 4 = ___

Test Prep

Fill in the O for the correct answer. NH means Not Here.

13. Find the missing number.

8 + □ = 14

14 − 8 = __?__

14	8	6	NH
○	○	○	○

Use with text pages 65–66.

Name ______________________ Date ______________

Write a Number Sentence

Write a number sentence to solve.

Draw or write to explain.

1. 9 girls and 8 boys twirl streamers in the parade. How many children twirl streamers in the parade?

   ____ + ____ = ____

   ____ children

2. There are 8 children marching in the jazz band. 3 of them play trumpets. How many children play other instruments?

   ____ − ____ = ____

   ____ children

3. 17 children dance with umbrellas in the parade. 8 umbrellas are yellow. The others are pink. How many umbrellas are pink?

   ____ − ____ = ____

   ____ pink umbrellas

Test Prep

Fill in the ○ for the correct answer. NH means Not Here.

4. Choose the number sentence.

   There are 9 children in the drum band. 4 children play congas. How many children play other kinds of drums?

9 − 7 =	9 + 4 =	9 − 4 =	NH
○	○	○	○

Use with text pages 67–69.

Name ______________________ Date ______________

Practice 4.1

Activity: Take a Survey

Sarah took a survey of her classmates.
Tim took a survey of his classmates.

Sarah's Class

Favorite color	Tally Marks
Blue	𝍷𝍷𝍷
Red	𝍸
Green	𝍷
Orange	
Yellow	𝍷𝍷

Tim's Class

Favorite color	Tally Marks
Blue	𝍷𝍷𝍷𝍷
Red	𝍸 𝍷
Green	
Orange	𝍷𝍷
Yellow	𝍷𝍷

Use the data in the charts to answer the questions.

1. Which color is the favorite in both classes?

   red

2. In whose class did more children choose blue?

   ____

3. Which color is liked by the same number of children?

   ____

4. Which color is liked by the fewest children?

   ____

5. How many children altogether like red?

   ______________ children

6. How many children did Tim survey?

   ____

Test Prep

Fill in the ○ for the correct answer. NH means Not Here.

7. Which tally shows 6 children were surveyed?

𝍸 𝍷	𝍷𝍷𝍷𝍷	𝍸 𝍷𝍷	NH
○	○	○	○

Use with text pages 77–79.

Name ______________________ Date __________

Practice 4.2

Read a Pictograph

The table shows what games the children like to play during recess.

<table>
<tr><th colspan="4">Recess Games</th></tr>
<tr><th>Simon Says</th><th>Jump rope</th><th>Catch</th><th>Soccer</th></tr>
<tr><td>||||</td><td>𝍸 |||</td><td>𝍸 |</td><td>𝍸 𝍸 ||</td></tr>
</table>

1. Use the table to make a pictograph.

   Draw 1 ☺ for every 2 children.

Recess Games	
Simon Says	☺ ☺
Jump rope	
Catch	
Soccer	
Key: Each ☺ stands for 2 children.	

Use the information in the pictograph to answer the question.

2. How many more children like playing soccer than Simon Says?

   _____ more children

3. If 4 more children say they like catch best, how many ☺ will you add to the pictograph? _____ ☺

Test Prep

Fill in the ○ for the correct answer. NH means Not Here.

4. Each ☆ stands for 2 children.

   What number does ☆ ☆ ☆ stand for?

8	6	3	NH
○	○	○	○

Use with text pages 81–82.

Name ______________________________ Date ______________

Practice 4.3

Activity: Make and Read Bar Graphs

Make a bar graph from the data below.

1. Miguel sells school supplies. He sold 1 backpack. He sold 2 more books than backpacks. He sold 4 more T-shirts than backpacks.

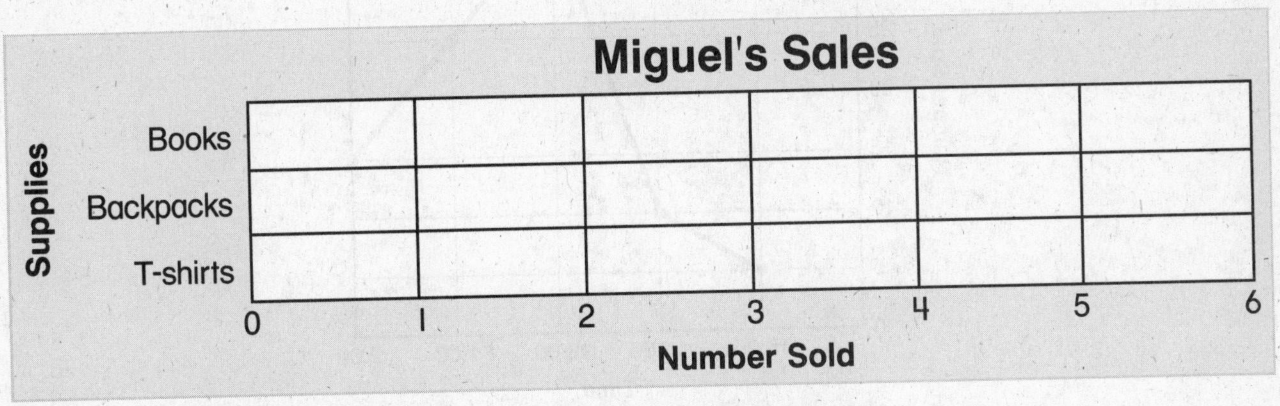

Use the data in the graph to answer the questions.

2. How many books did Miguel sell?

_____ books

3. How many T-shirts did Miguel sell?

_____ T-shirts

4. What did Miguel sell the fewest of?

____

5. What is the total number of school supplies Miguel sold?

_____

Test Prep

Fill in the ○ for the correct answer. NH means Not Here.

6. Each colored box on a bar graph stands for 2 children. How many boxes must be colored to show 6 children?

8	6	3	NH
○	○	○	○

Name ______________________ Date ______________

Practice 4.4

Line Graphs

A line graph shows how something changes over time.

Look at the graph below. The left side of the line graph shows the number of sandwiches sold. The bottom of the graph shows the different times of day.

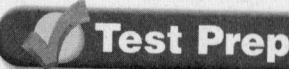

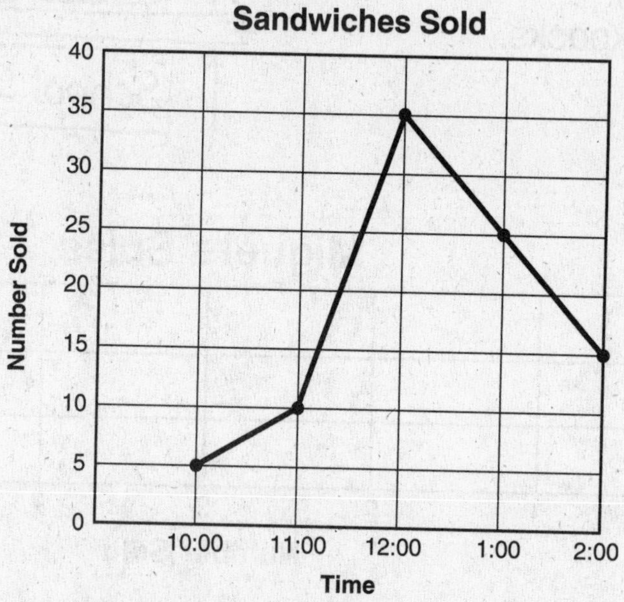

Use the line graph to answer the question.

1. At what time were the most sandwiches sold?

____

2. How many more sandwiches were sold at 11:00 than 10:00?

____

Test Prep

Fill in the ○ for the correct answer. NH means Not Here.

3. How many sandwiches were sold at 2:00?

10	35	15	NH
○	○	○	○

Name ______________________ Date ____________

Practice 4.5

Graphing on a Coordinate Grid

Find the objects on the grid.
Write the ordered pair.

(5, 4) means move 5 spaces to the right. Then move 4 spaces up.

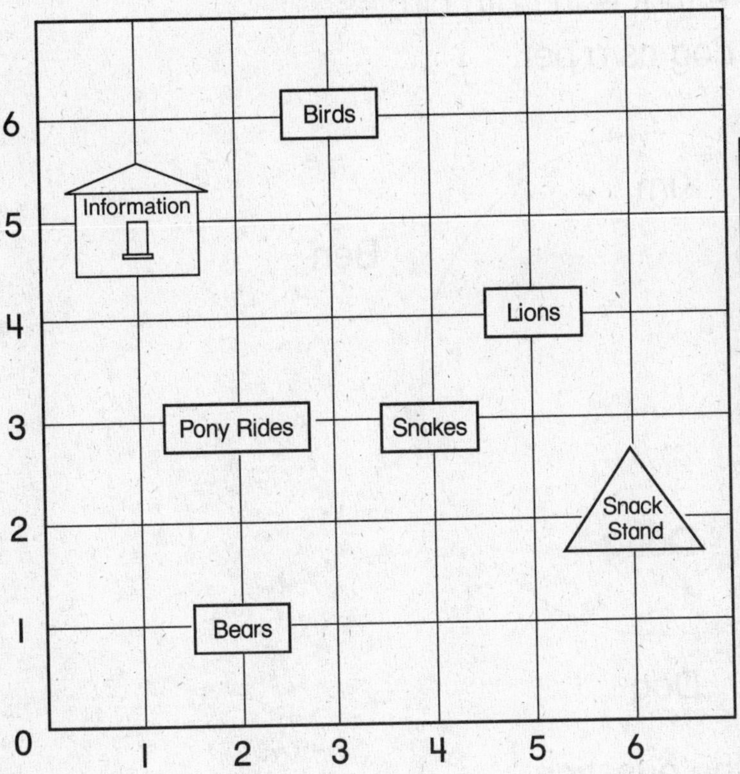

Place	Ordered pair
1. Lions	(5, 4)
2. Birds	(____, ____)
3. Information Booth	(____, ____)
4. Snakes	(____, ____)
5. Bears	(____, ____)

6. What place would you find at (6, 2)?

____

Test Prep

Fill in the ○ for the correct answer. NH means Not Here.

7. On a grid, point (5, 5) is located _____ point (5, 4).

next to	above	below	NH
○	○	○	○

Use with text pages 89–90.

Name ________________________ Date ____________

Venn Diagrams

The Venn diagram below shows the kind of pets that Jasmine's friends have. One circle shows her friends who have a cat for a pet. The other circle shows the friends who have a dog. The name that is in both circles is the friend who has a cat and a dog as a pet.

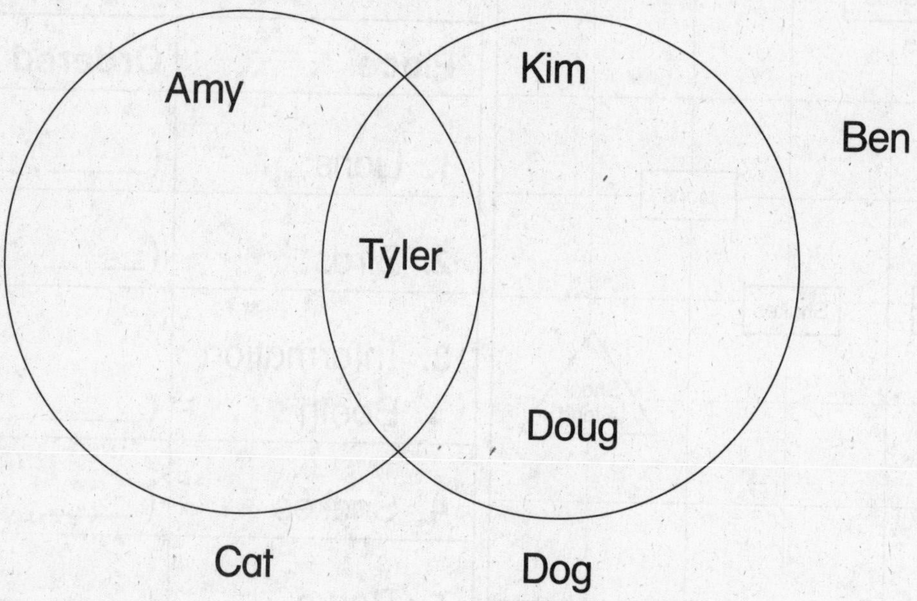

Use the Venn diagram to answer the question.

1. How many of Jasmine's friends have a dog for a pet? _____ children

2. Which friend does not have a cat or a dog as a pet? _________

3. How many of Jasmine's friends have a cat for a pet? _____ children

Test Prep

Fill in the ○ for the correct answer. NH means Not Here.

4. Jon has a dog for a pet. His name belongs in the circle with which person?

   Amy ○ Tyler ○ Doug ○ NH ○

Name ______________________ Date ____________

Practice 4.7

More Likely, Less Likely, Equally Likely

You can tell if an event is more likely, less likely, or equally likely to happen.

1. 7 red cubes and 5 blue cubes are in a bag. How likely are you to pick a red cube rather than a blue cube?

   more likely   less likely   equally likely

2. Place 7 red cubes and 5 blue cubes in a bag. Pick one cube from a bag. Record the color. Return the cube to the bag.

Color	Times Picked (10 picks in all)
Red	
Blue	

3. 3 red cubes and 9 blue cubes are in a bag. How likely are you to pick a red cube rather than a blue cube?

   more likely   less likely   equally likely

4. Place 3 red cubes and 9 blue cubes in a bag. Pick one cube from a bag. Record the color. Return the cube to the bag.

Color	Times Picked (10 picks in all)
Red	
Blue	

Test Prep

Fill in the ○ for the correct answer. NH means Not Here.

5. An event that is likely to happen is ____.

   impossible ○   probable ○   certain ○   NH ○

Use with text pages 95–97.

Name ______________________ Date ______________

Practice 4.8

Activity: Predicting Outcomes

When you predict the outcome of an event, you tell what will most likely happen.

1. Predict the color the spinner will land on most often. white

Use a paper clip and pencil.
Spin 15 times. Record your spins.

Color	Tally
White	
Gray	
Black	

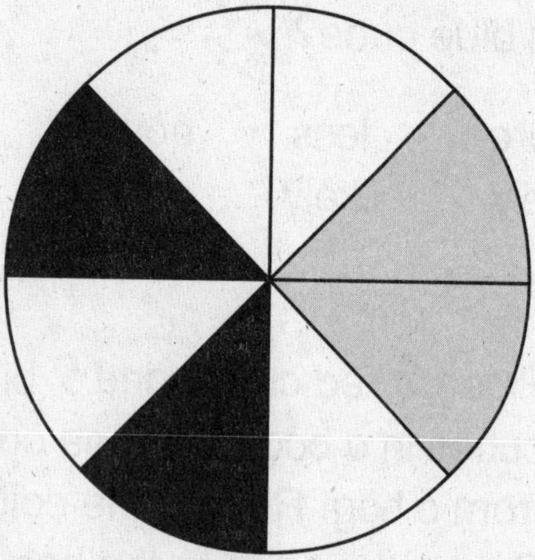

2. Which color did you land on most often?

____

____

3. Use three colors to color the parts of this spinner. Use blue to color the part the spinner would land on most often.

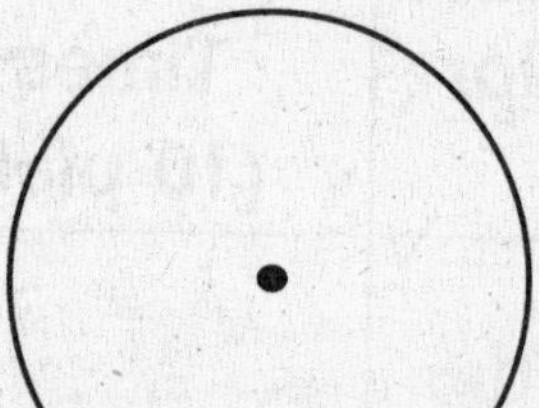

Test Prep

Fill in the ○ for the correct answer. NH means Not Here.

4. May spins this spinner 10 times. Which number do you think she will spin most often?

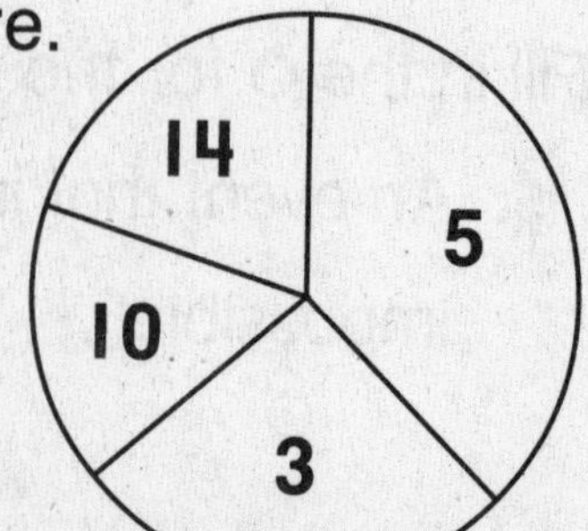

10 ○ 5 ○ 3 ○ NH ○

Use with text pages 99–100.

Name ____________________ Date ____________

Problem Solving: Use a Graph

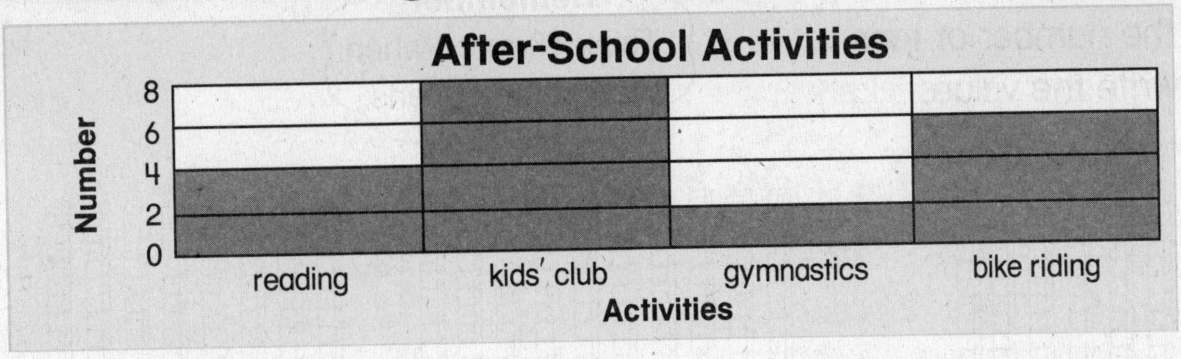

Use the data in the graph to solve.

Draw or write to explain.

1. How many children read?

   4 children

2. How many children altogether do bike riding and gymnastics?

   _____ children

3. How many more children are in the kids' club than read?

   _____ children

4. Which activity do children do the least?

   ____

Test Prep

Fill in the ○ for the correct answer. NH means Not Here.

5. Justin makes a bar graph. He shows that 9 children like soccer, 4 children like hockey, and 3 children like skating. Which sport has the longest bar?

hockey	skating	soccer	NH
○	○	○	○

Use with text pages 101–103.

Name ______________________ Date ____________

Practice 5.1

Tens Through 100

Write the number of tens.
Then write the value.

Remember
Think 10 more when you count by tens.

1.

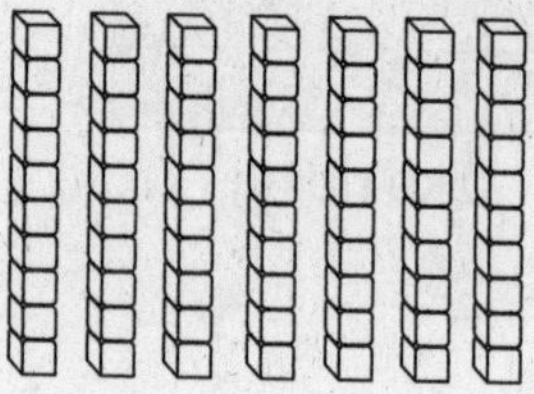

7 tens

70

seventy

2.

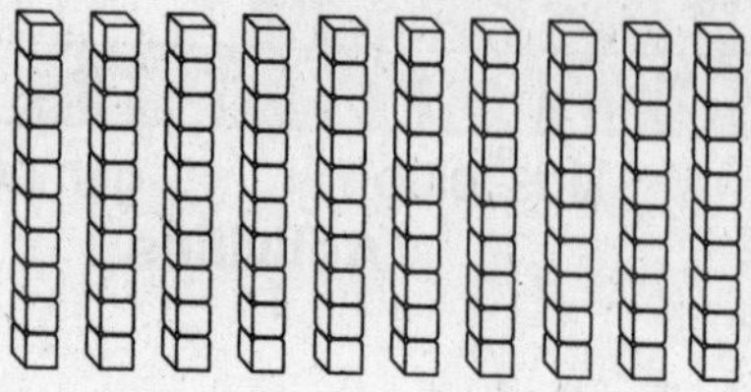

______ tens

______

one hundred

3.

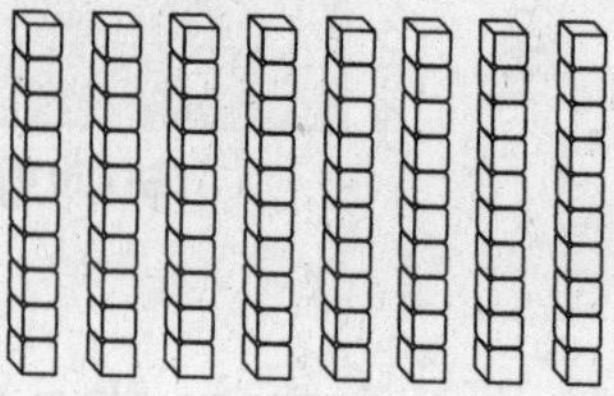

______ tens

______

eighty

4.

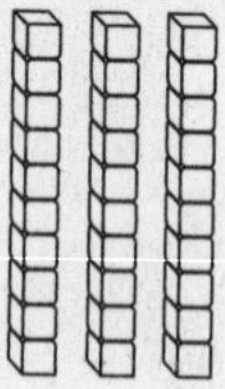

______ tens

______

thirty

5.

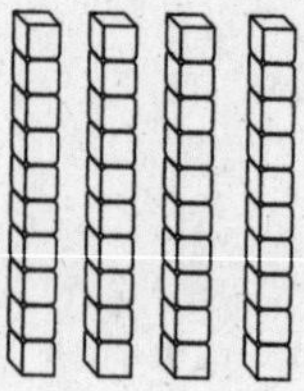

______ tens

______

forty

6.

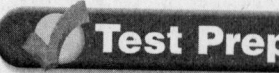

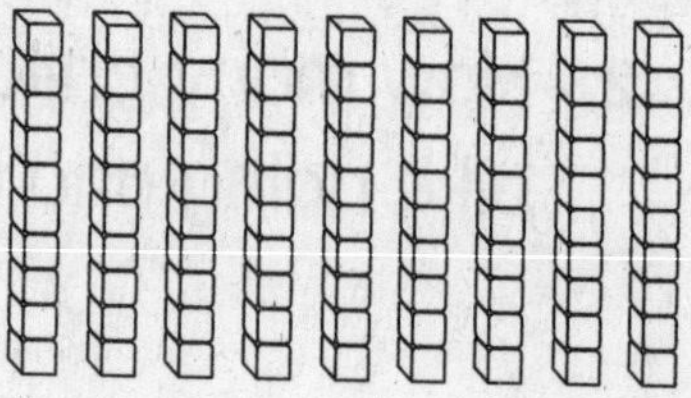

______ tens

______

ninety

Write the missing numbers.

7. 10, 20, ______, 40

8. ______, 50, ______, 70, 80

9. 70, ______, 50, ______, 30

Test Prep

Fill in the ○ for the correct answer. NH means Not Here.

10. How many tens are in 50?

50	5	0	NH
○	○	○	○

Use with text pages 125–126.

Name ______________________ Date ____________

Practice 5.2

Tens and Ones to 100

Write the tens and ones.
Write the numbers.

1. 4 tens 5 ones

Tens	Ones
4	5

45

forty-five

2. 9 tens 2 ones

Tens	Ones

_____

ninety-two

3. 5 tens 3 ones

Tens	Ones

_____

fifty-three

4. 7 tens 0 ones

Tens	Ones

_____

seventy

5. 2 tens 6 ones

Tens	Ones

_____

twenty-six

6. 1 ten 8 ones

Tens	Ones

_____

eighteen

Test Prep

Fill in the ○ for the correct answer. NH means Not Here.

7. Which shows the number in words?

Tens	Ones
8	3

eighty-three ○ thirty-eight ○ five ○ NH ○

Name _____ Date _____

Identify Place Value

Complete the chart.

Remember
To find the value of a digit, find the value of its place.

Count how many.	Write the tens and ones.	Write the value of each digit.	Write the number.
1.	_3_ tens _2_ ones	____ + ____	____
2.	___ tens ___ ones	____ + ____	____

Circle the value of the underlined digit.

3. <u>6</u>7

 60 6

4. 9<u>8</u>

 80 8

5. <u>2</u>3

 20 2

6. <u>4</u>4

 40 4

7. <u>8</u>5

 80 8

8. 7<u>1</u>

 10 1

Solve.

9. I have fewer ones than tens. The value of my tens is 20.
 What two numbers can I be? _____

Test Prep

Fill in the ○ for the correct answer. NH means Not Here.

10. Which number has the value of 2 tens and 9 ones?

 92 79 29 NH
 ○ ○ ○ ○

Use with text pages 129–130.

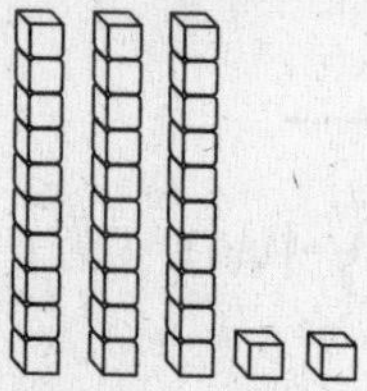

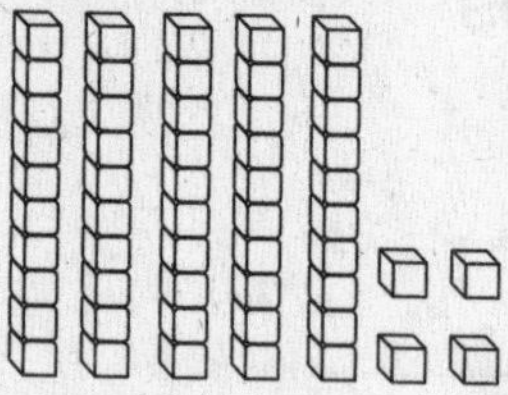

Name ______________________ Date ____________

Practice 5.4

Different Ways to Show Numbers

Circle two ways to make the number.

1. 68 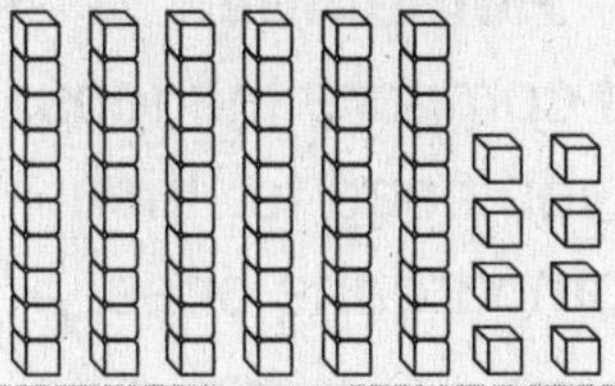 8 tens 6 ones 60 + 8

2. 31 30 + 1 1 ten 3 ones 

3. 57 5 tens 7 ones 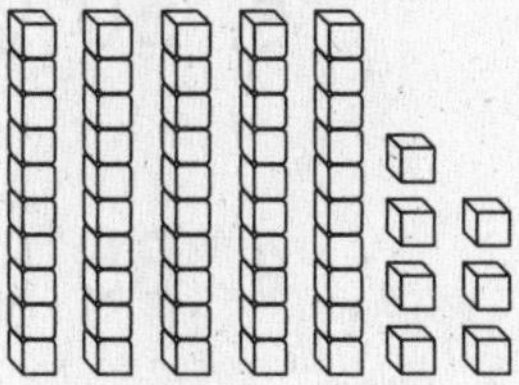 5 + 70

4. 14 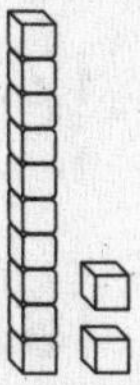 10 + 4 

5. 26 20 + 6 20 + 60 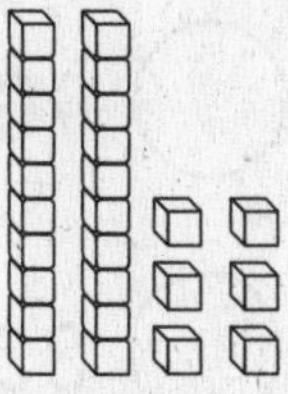

6. 72 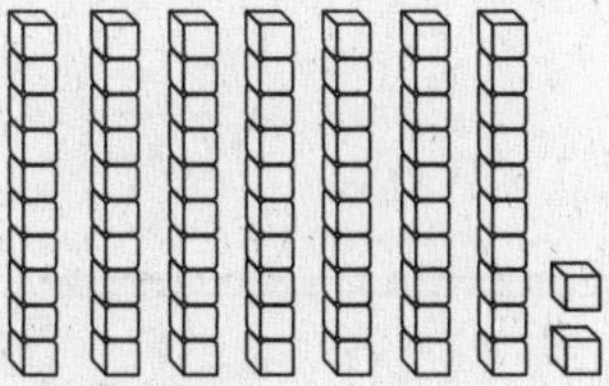 7 tens 2 ones 2 tens 7 ones

Test Prep

Fill in the ○ for the correct answer. NH means Not Here.

7. Which shows another way to make 29?

20 tens 9 ones	2 tens 9 ones	29 tens	NH
○	○	○	○

Use with text pages 133–134.

Name ______________________ Date ______________

Practice 5.5

Compare Two-Digit Numbers

Remember
First compare the tens.
If you need to, then
compare the ones.

Write >, <, or =.

1. 52 (>) 23	**2.** 81 ◯ 96	**3.** 25 ◯ 32
4. 32 ◯ 12	**5.** 50 ◯ 70	**6.** 48 ◯ 27
7. 61 ◯ 72	**8.** 85 ◯ 85	**9.** 94 ◯ 99
10. 93 ◯ 63	**11.** 30 ◯ 39	**12.** 18 ◯ 25
13. 52 ◯ 52	**14.** 75 ◯ 71	**15.** 56 ◯ 46
16. 91 ◯ 90	**17.** 28 ◯ 28	**18.** 45 ◯ 51
19. 37 ◯ 33	**20.** 65 ◯ 64	**21.** 10 ◯ 20

Test Prep

Fill in the ○ for the correct answer. NH means Not Here.

22. Compare the numbers. Choose the symbol.

68 ◯ 76

>	<	=	NH
○	○	○	○

Use with text pages 135–136.

Name ____________________ Date ____________

Practice 5.6

Problem Solving: Reasonable Answers

Circle the most reasonable answer.

Draw or write to explain.

1. This year Brad invited 15 friends to a skating party. Last year he invited fewer friends. How many friends did he invite last year?

   12 friends   18 friends   20 friends

2. The Swim Club has 20 children. The Make-a-Mask Club has a few more children. How many children are in the Make-a-Mask Club?

   16 children   25 children   80 children

3. Tan can juggle 5 balls. Nela can juggle even more. How many balls can Nela juggle?

   3 balls   7 balls   24 balls

Test Prep

Fill in the ○ for the correct answer. NH means Not Here.
Choose the most reasonable answer.

4. Max collects baseball cards. He has 27 cards. He sold some of them to get spending money. How many cards might Max have left?

29	27	20	26
○	○	○	○

Use with text pages 137–138.

Name ______________________ Date ______________

Even and Odd Numbers

Use cubes or draw dots.
Make groups of two to show the number.
Circle **even** or **odd**.

Remember
You can make groups of 2 to tell if a number is even or odd.

1. 16 even odd
2. 22 even odd
3. 27 even odd
4. 20 even odd
5. 18 even odd
6. 12 even odd
7. 13 even odd
8. 23 even odd

9. Color the even numbers Red.
Color the odd numbers Blue.

15	16	17	18	19	20

Test Prep

Fill in the ○ for the correct answer. NH means Not Here.

10. Which is an odd number?

8 ○ 10 ○ 13 ○ NH ○

Use with text pages 145–146.

Name ______________________ Date ______________

Practice 6.2

Activity: Skip Counting

Use the hundred chart.

Remember
When you skip count on a hundred chart, the numbers follow a pattern.

1	2	3	4	5			8		10
11				15	16			19	
21	22			25		27	28		
31		33					38		40
	42				46	47		49	
	52		54			57		59	
61	62	63	64	65	66	67	68	69	70
71	72	73	74	75	76	77	78	79	80
81	82	83	84	85	86	87	88	89	90
91	92	93	94	95	96	97	98	99	100

1. Write the missing numbers.

2. Count by 5s.
Circle the numbers.

3. Count by 3s. Put an X on the numbers.

Follow the pattern.
Write the missing numbers.

4. 18, 21, 24, 27, _____, 33, _____

Test Prep

Fill in the ○ for the correct answer. NH means Not Here.

5. Continue the pattern. What is the next number?

30, 34, 38, 42, _____

44	48	52	NH
○	○	○	○

Use with text pages 147–148.

Name ______________________ Date ____________

Practice 6.3

Order Two-Digit Numbers to 100

Use the number line.

> **Remember**
> A number line can help you find a number that comes just before, between, or just after.

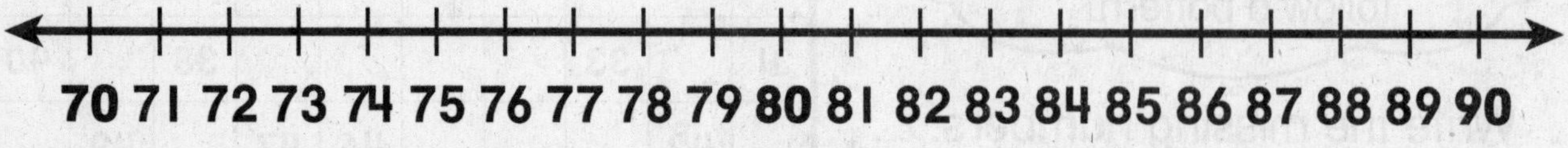

Write the number that comes just after.

1. 72, 73, 74 2. 81, 82, ____ 3. 78, 79, ____

Write the number that comes just before.

4. ____, 78, 79 5. ____, 81, 82 6. ____, 71, 72

Write the number that comes between.

7. 88, ____, 90 8. 77, ____, 79 9. 85, ____, 87

Write the missing numbers.

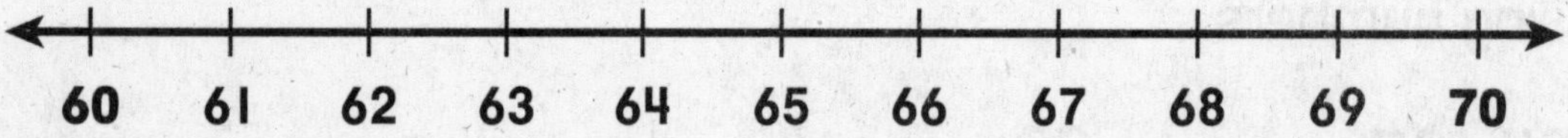

10. 69, 68, ____, 66, ____, 64, ____, 62, 61

11. What number is just after 69? ____

Test Prep

Fill in the ○ for the correct answer. NH means Not Here.

12. What number comes between 76 and 78?

75 ○ 77 ○ 79 ○ NH ○

Use with text pages 149–150.

Name ______________________ Date ____________

Practice 6.4

Ordinal Numbers

You use ordinal numbers to tell the position of things.
Use the picture. Circle the answer.

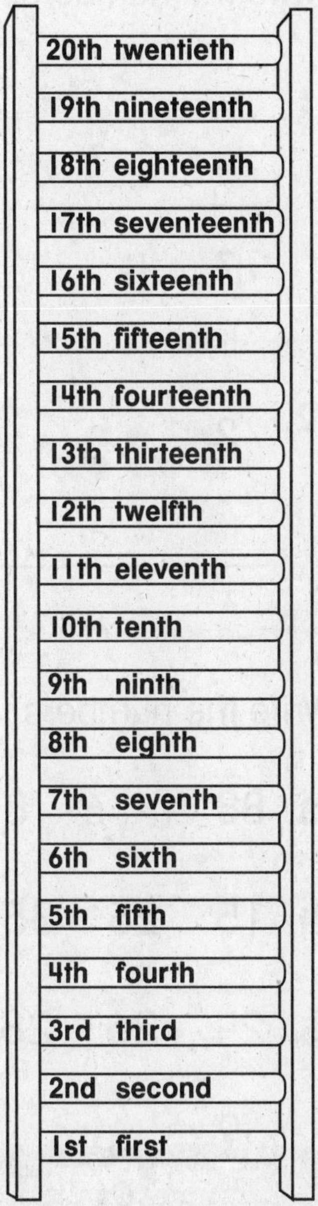

1. Which step is just below the twelfth step?

   13th 11th 12th

2. Which step is just above the 18th step?

   eighteenth seventeenth nineteenth

3. Which step is between the fourteenth step and the sixteenth step?

   15th 17th 13th

4. Which step is just above the bottom step?

   twentieth second nineteenth

5. Which step is just below the top step?

   19th 20th 1st

Test Prep

Fill in the ○ for the correct answer. NH means Not Here.

6. How many steps are between the 8th step and the 11th step?

   1 ○ 2 ○ 3 ○ NH ○

Use with text pages 151–153.

Name ______________________ Date ______________

Practice 6.5

Repeating and Growing Patterns

Draw the next picture to continue the pattern.
Write the numbers.

1. 

1 4 __7__ __10__ __13__

2. 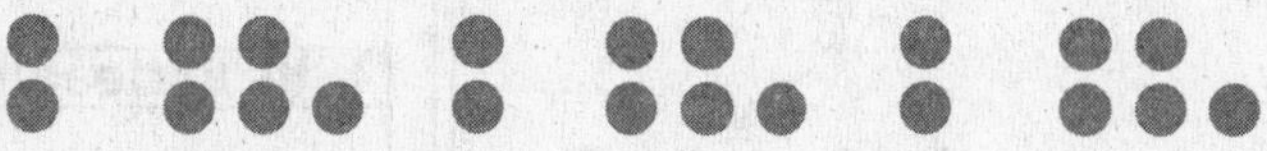

____ ____ ____ ____ ____ ____ ____

Write the numbers to continue the pattern.

3. 8 4 6 8 4 6 8 4 6 ____

4. 15 25 35 45 55 ____ ____

5. 24 26 28 30 32 ____ ____

Test Prep

Fill in the ○ for the correct answer. NH means Not Here.

6. Which letter pattern is like the shape pattern?

ABAB	ABCABC	AAAA	NH
○	○	○	○

Use with text pages 155–156.

Name ______________________ Date ____________

Practice 6.6

Problem Solving: Find a Pattern

Look for the pattern. Then solve.

Draw or write to explain.

1. 2 horses are needed to pull each cart. How many horses are needed to pull 5 carts?

Carts	1	2	3	4	5
Horses	2	4	6	8	10

______ horses

2. Each clown has 4 balloons. How many balloons do 6 clowns have?

Clowns	1	2	3	4	5	6
Balloons	4	8				

______ balloons

3. There are 5 acrobats in each row. How many acrobats are in 7 rows?

Rows	1	2	3	4	5	6	7
Acrobats	5	10	15				

______ acrobats

Test Prep

Fill in the ○ for the correct answer. NH means Not Here.

4. Find the pattern. Solve.

Each clown has 3 hats in a bag.
How many hats are in 4 bags?

6	9	12	NH
○	○	○	○

Use with text pages 157–159.

Name ______________________ Date ____________

Sides and Vertices of Plane Shapes

Match the objects and the sentences.

1. It has 0 sides.

2. It has 4 sides.

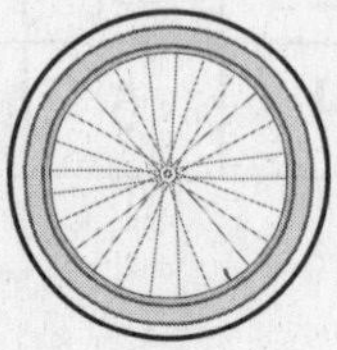

3. It has 3 sides.

Write the name of the shape.
Write two reasons for your answer.

square rectangle circle hexagon triangle trapezoid

4.

____

____

____

5.

____

____

____

Test Prep

Fill in the ○ for the correct answer. NH means Not Here.

6. Which shape has four sides that are the same?

triangle	rectangle	square	NH
○	○	○	○

Use with text pages 181–182.

Name ______________________ Date ______________

Practice 7.2

Angles

Look at the angle.

Write **obtuse, acute, or right.**

1.

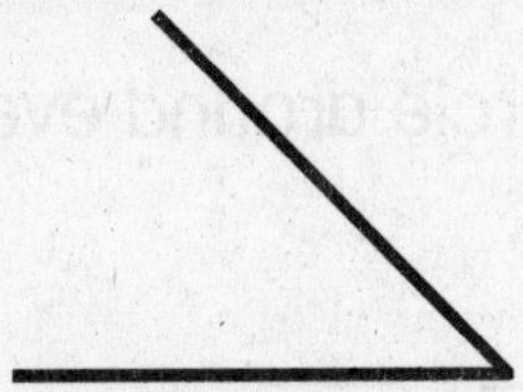

acute angle

2.

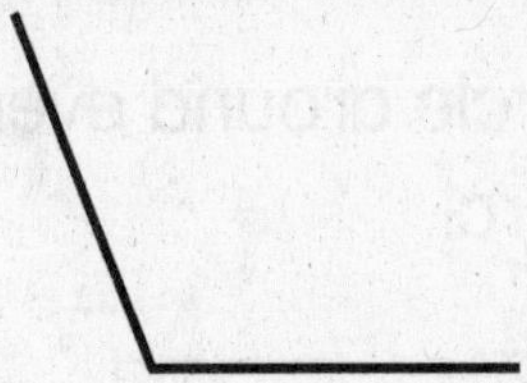

__________ angle

3.

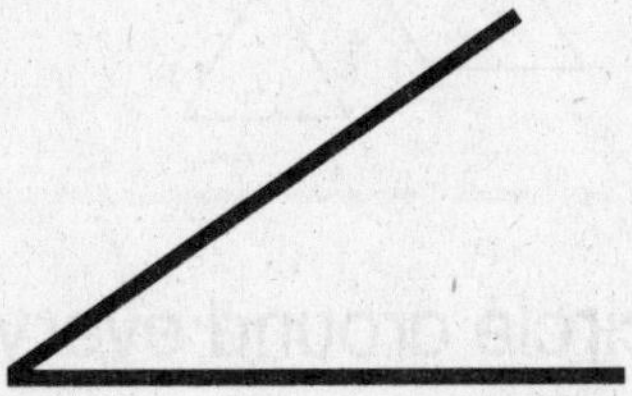

__________ angle

4.

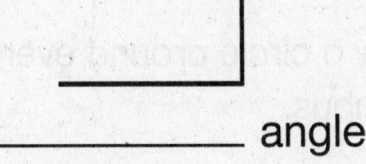

__________ angle

5.

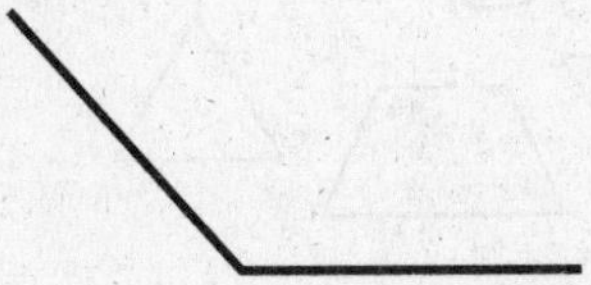

__________ angle

6.

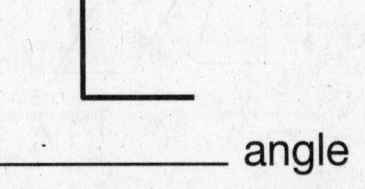

__________ angle

Test Prep

Fill in the ○ for the correct answer. NH means Not Here.

7. What kind of an angle is shown in the figure?

Acute	Obtuse	Right	NH
○	○	○	○

Use with text pages 183–184.

Name ______________________ Date ____________

Quadrilaterals

A quadrilateral has 4 sides. Parallelograms are special kinds of quadrilaterals.

1. Draw a circle around every quadrilateral.

2. Draw a circle around every trapezoid.

3. Draw a circle around every rhombus.

4. Draw a circle around every parallelogram.

Test Prep

Fill in the ○ for the correct answer. NH means Not Here.

5. Name the figure.

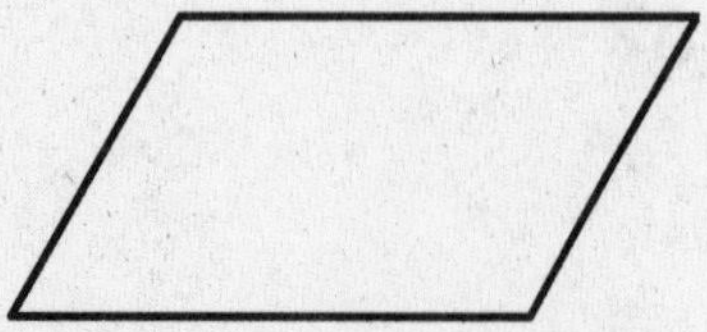

rhombus ○ parallelogram ○ square ○ NH ○

Use with text pages 185–186.

Name ______________________ Date ____________

Practice 7.4

Combine and Separate Shapes

Use pattern blocks to make Shape A.
Then, change the blocks to make a new shape. Trace the blocks.

Use these blocks.	Shape A	New Shape
1. 2 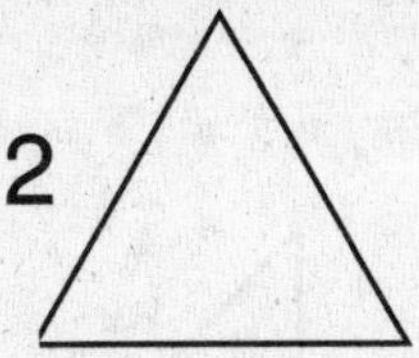	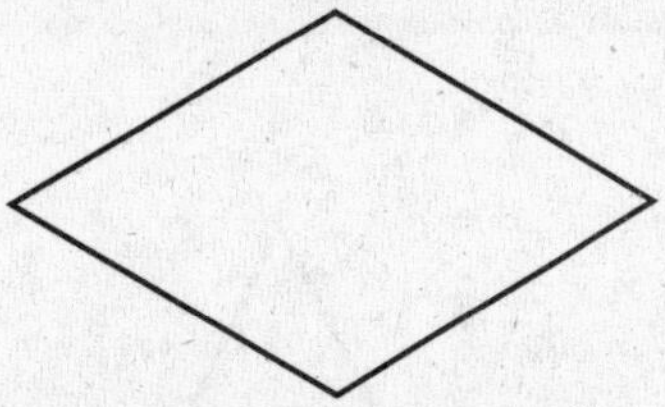	
2. 3 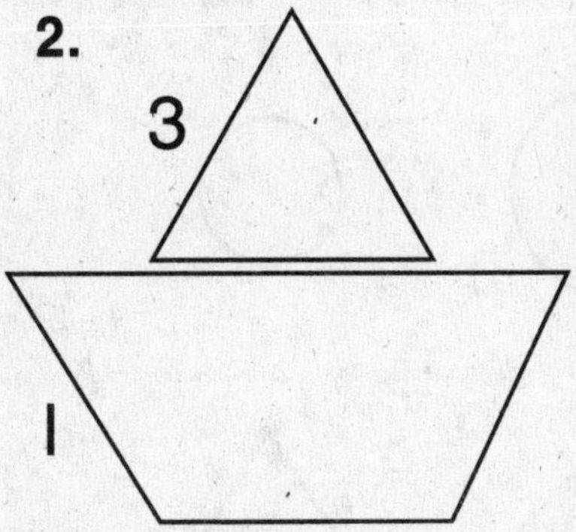 1	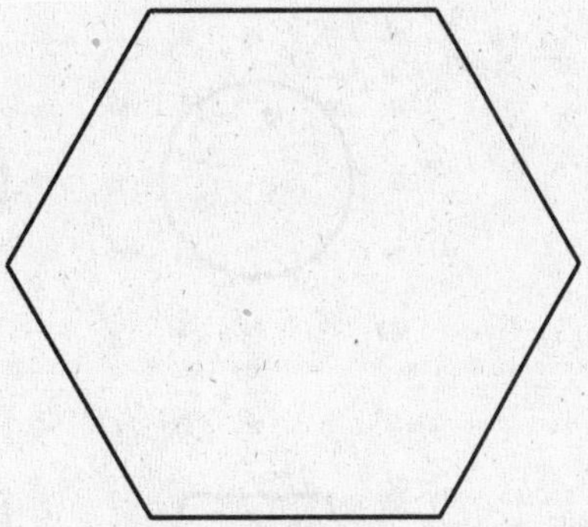	
3. 4 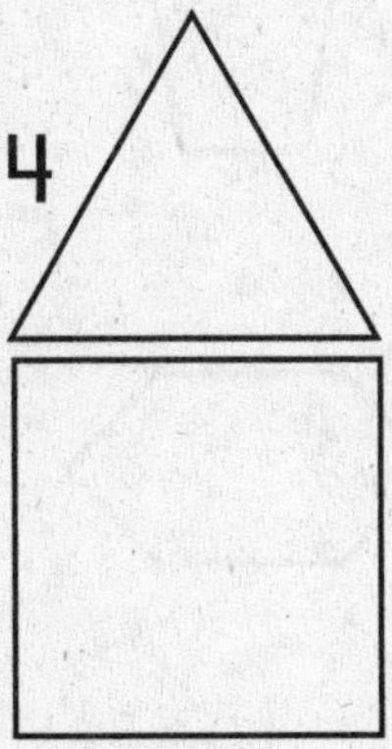 1	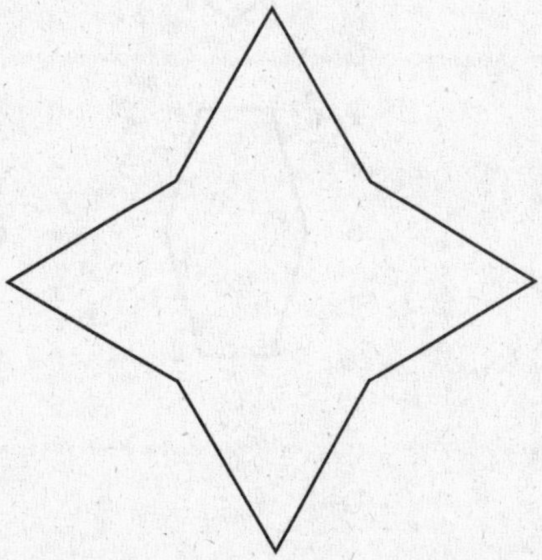	

Test Prep

Fill in the ○ for the correct answer. NH means Not Here.

4. What shape can you make with 2  ?

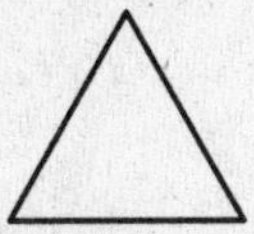 ○ 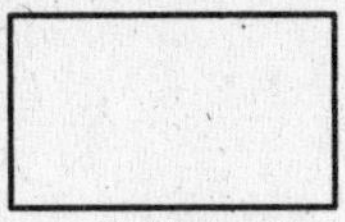 ○ 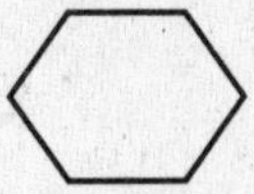 ○ NH ○

Use with text pages 187–189.

Name ______________________ Date ______________

Practice 7.5

Congruent Shapes

Remember
Congruent shapes are the same size and shape.

Circle the shape that is congruent to the first shape.

1. 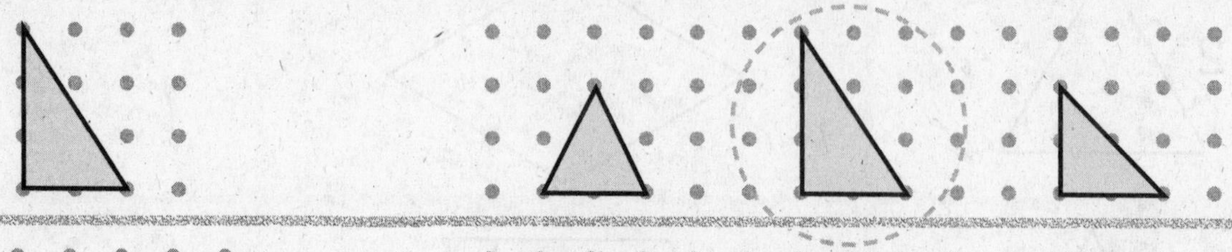

2. 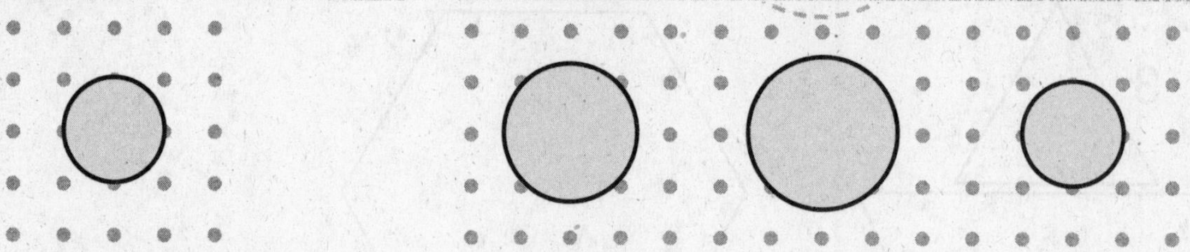

3. 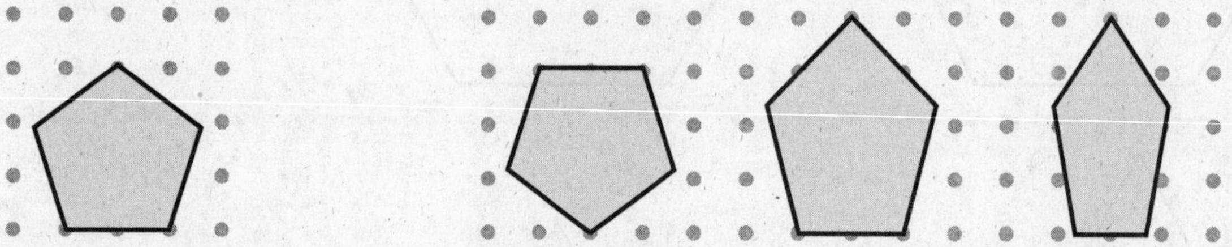

4. 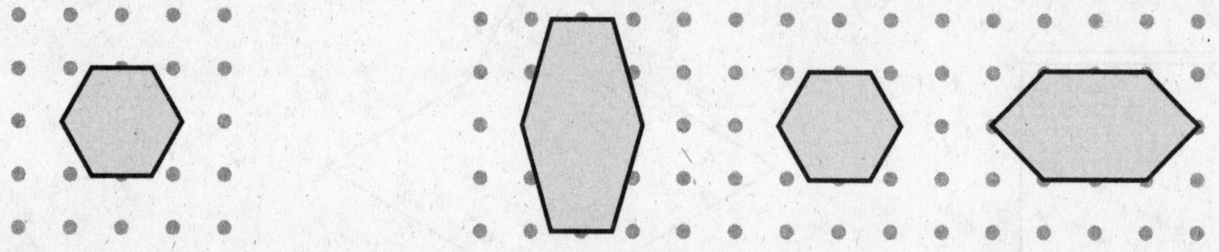

Test Prep

Fill in the ○ for the correct answer. NH means Not Here.

5. Which shape is congruent to the triangle?

○ ○ ○ ○ NH

Use with text pages 191–192.

Name ______________________ Date ______________

Practice 7.6

Activity: Symmetry

Circle the shape if it has a line of symmetry.
Draw a line of symmetry.

1. W	2. 5	3. V
4. F	5. 3	6. M
7. 9	8. H	9. O
10. D	11. 7	12. X

Test Prep

Fill in the ○ for the correct answer. NH means Not Here.

13. Which shape shows a correctly drawn line of symmetry?

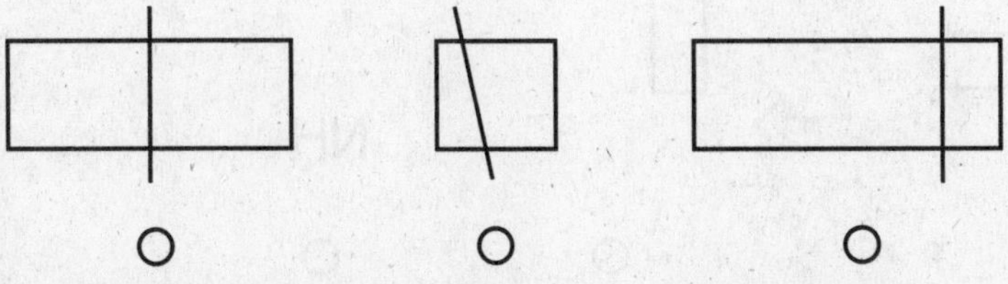

○ ○ ○ NH ○

Name ______________________ Date ____________

Practice 7.7

Slides, Flips, and Turns

Move the shape. Trace to show the move.

Remember
You can move shapes in different ways.

1. slide

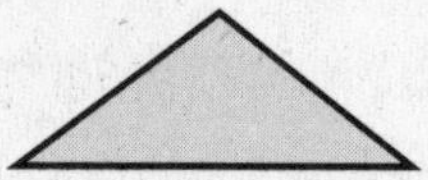

2. flip

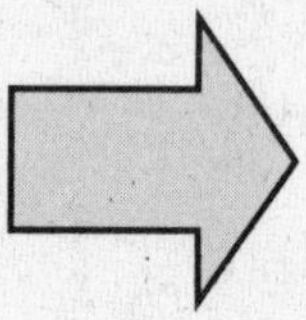

3. turn

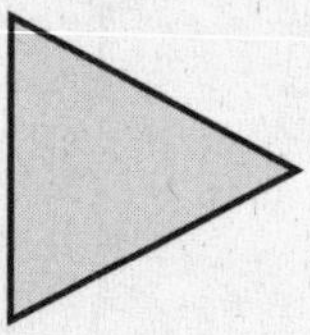

4. flip

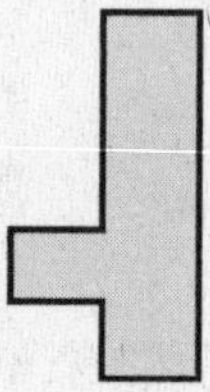

Test Prep

Fill in the ○ for the correct answer. NH means Not Here.

5. Which shape shows a slide?

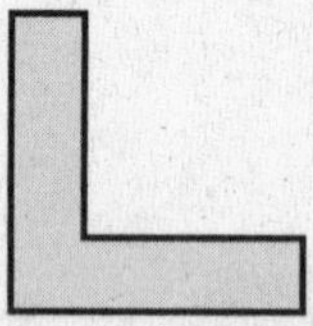

 ○

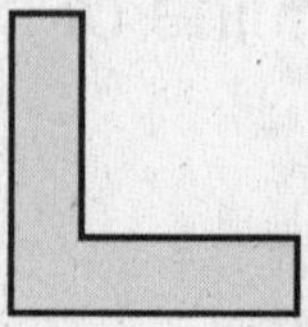 ○

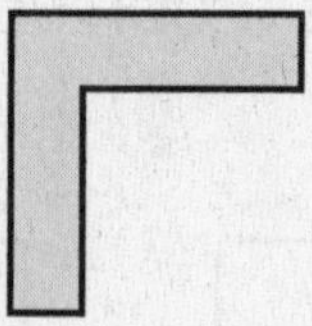 ○

NH ○

Use with text pages 197–198.

Name ______________________ Date ____________

Practice 7.8

Problem Solving: Find a Pattern

Look for the pattern.

Draw or write to explain.

1. Lucy drew a pattern on a card she was making. What two shapes are likely to come next?

______ ______

2. Ben is making a border for his poster. What two shapes are likely to come next?

______ ______

3. Millie is making some wrapping paper with a pattern. Here is the beginning of the pattern: a shape with four equal sides, a shape with three sides and a shape with no sides at all. Draw the first three shapes of the pattern.

______ ______ ______

Test Prep

Fill in the ○ for the correct answer. NH means Not Here.

4. What two shapes are likely to come next?

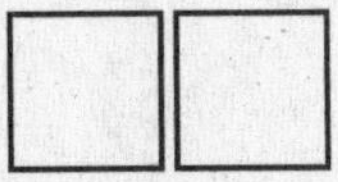

○

○

○

NH

○

Use with text pages 199–201.

Name ______________________ Date ____________

Practice 8.1

Identifying Solid Shapes

Write the names of the two solid shapes in the picture.

1.

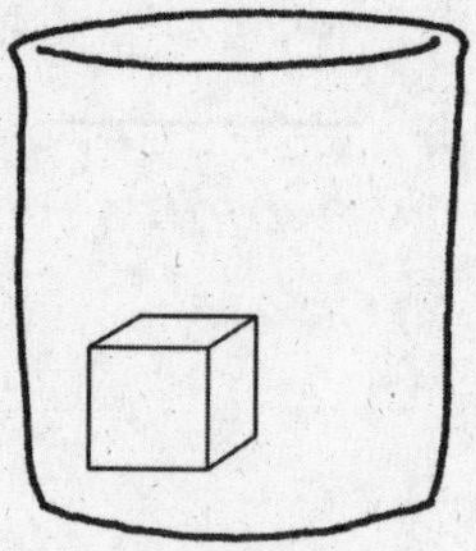

cube

cylinder

2.

____

____

3.

____

____

4.

____

____

Test Prep

Fill in the ○ for the correct answer. NH means Not Here.

5. Which object is an example of a cylinder?

ice-cream cone	soup can	cereal box	NH
○	○	○	○

Use with text pages 209–210.

Name ______________________ Date ____________

Practice 8.2

Faces, Edges, and Vertices

Circle the shapes that match the description.

1. 6 faces, 12 edges, 8 vertices

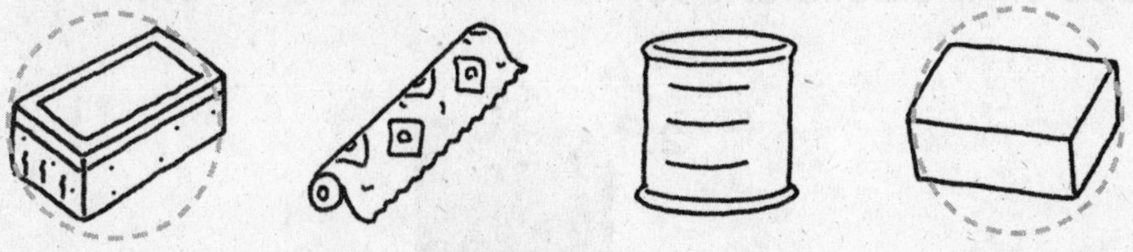

2. 1 face, 0 edges, 1 vertex

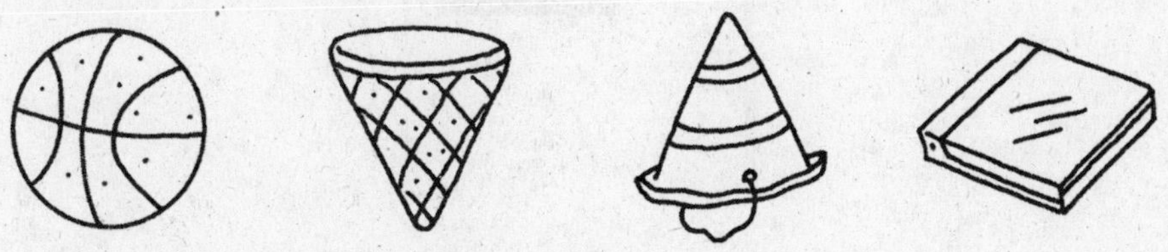

3. 0 faces, 0 edges, 0 vertices

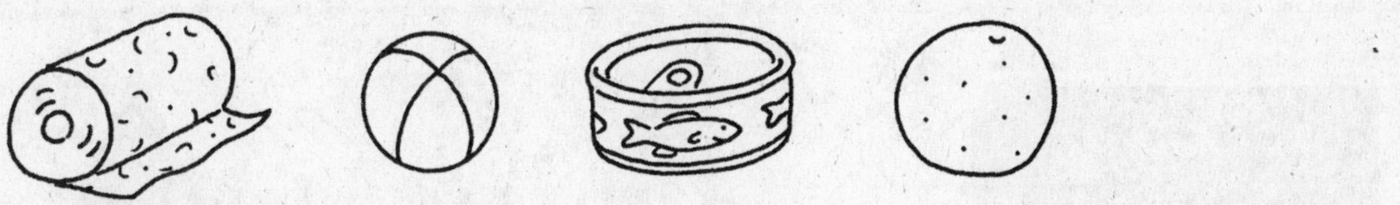

4. 6 faces, 12 edges, 8 vertices

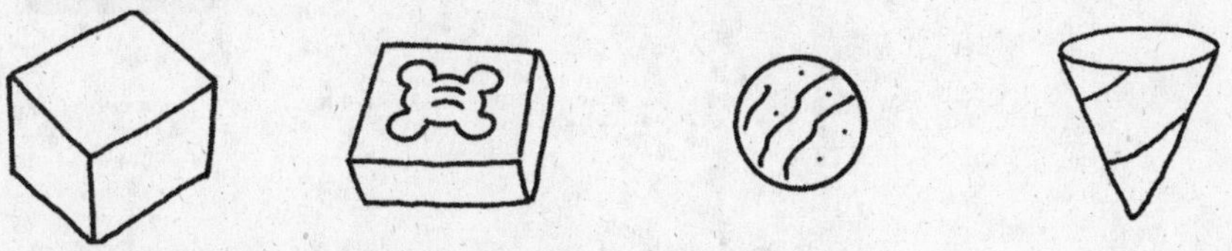

5. 2 faces, 0 edges, 0 vertices

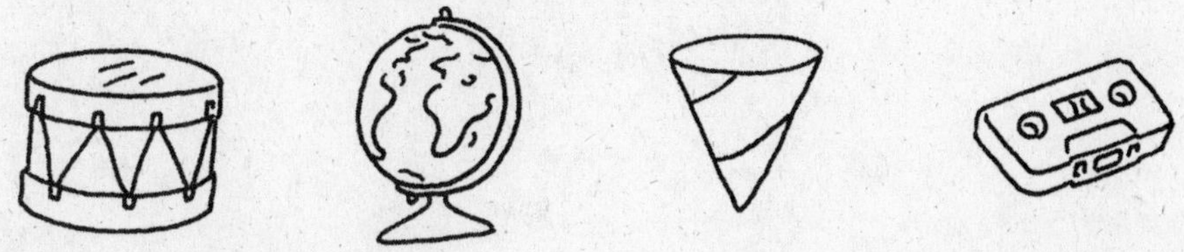

Test Prep

Fill in the ○ for the correct answer. NH means Not Here.

6. Which solid does not roll?

cone	sphere	square pyramid	NH
○	○	○	○

Use with text pages 211–212.

Name ______________________________ Date ______________

Practice 8.3

Activity: Plane Shapes on Solid Shapes

Draw the plane shapes you would make
if you traced the faces on the solid shape.

1.

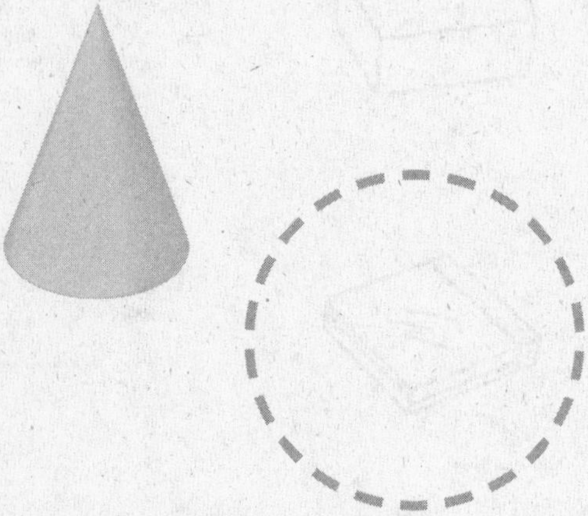

2.

3.

4.

Test Prep

Fill in the ○ for the correct answer. NH means Not Here.

5. Which solid shape will give you a circle when you trace a face?

cylinder	rectangular prism	sphere	NH
○	○	○	○

Use with text pages 213–214.

Name ______________________ Date ____________

Practice 8.4

Classify and Compare Solid Shapes

Remember
Count faces, edges, and vertices to compare solid shapes.

Write how the pair is alike or different.

		Alike	**Different**
1.		Both shapes have a square face.	A cube has 6 square faces; a square pyramid has 1 square face.
2.	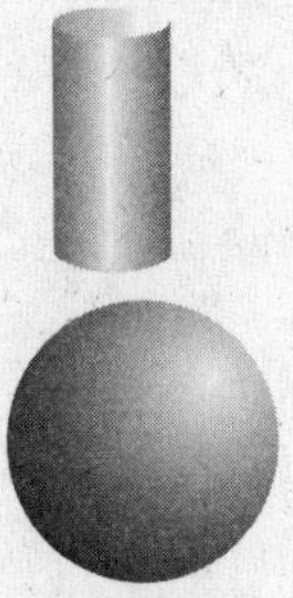	______	______
3.		______	______

Test Prep

Fill in the ○ for the correct answer. NH means Not Here.

4. Which shape does not roll or stack?

square pyramid	cube	cone	NH
○	○	○	○

Use with text pages 217–218.

Name ______________________ Date ____________

Practice 8.5

Problem Solving: Logical Thinking

Color	Number of Votes
blue	14
red	11
green	7
black	2

Each member of the team got to vote for a team color. Look at the results of the vote.

Use the table. Solve.

Draw or write to explain.

1. Anna chose the color that got more votes than green. Her color got an odd number of votes. Which color did Anna choose?

   ____

2. Daryl likes the color that got more than 2 votes. His color got an even number of votes. Which color did Daryl choose?

   ____

3. Sarah chose the color that got fewer than 14 votes. Her color got an even number of votes. Which color did Sarah choose? ____________

Test Prep

Fill in the ○ for the correct answer. NH means Not Here.

4. How many more votes than green did black and blue get?

5	9	12	NH
○	○	○	○

Use with text pages 219–221.

Name ______________________ Date ______________

Practice 9.1

Unit Fractions

Write the fraction for the shaded part.

1. 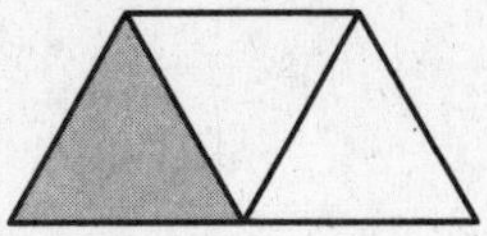

$\frac{1}{3}$

2. 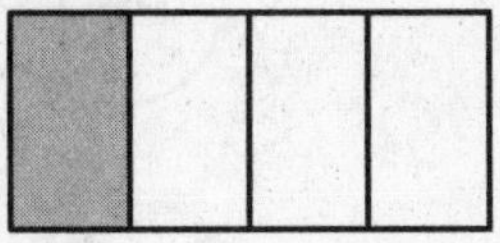

______

3. 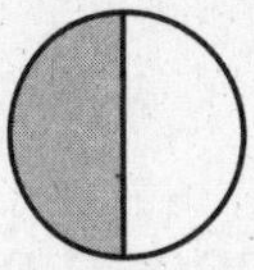

______

4. 

______

5. 

______

6. 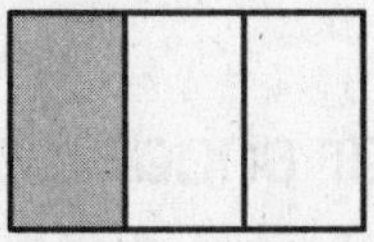

______

Color to show the fraction.

7. 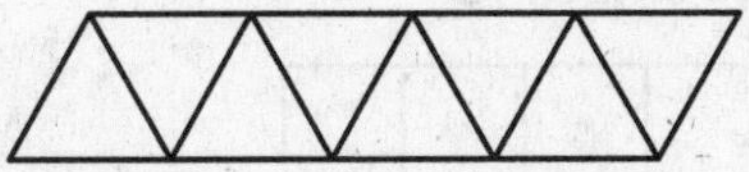

$\frac{1}{8}$

8. 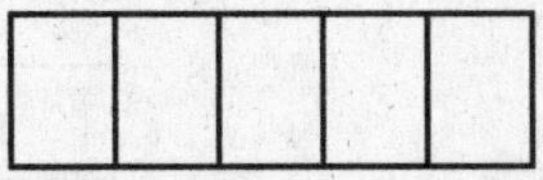

$\frac{1}{5}$

9. 

$\frac{1}{4}$

Test Prep

Fill in the ○ for the correct answer. NH means Not Here.

10. What is the fraction for the shaded part?

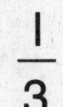

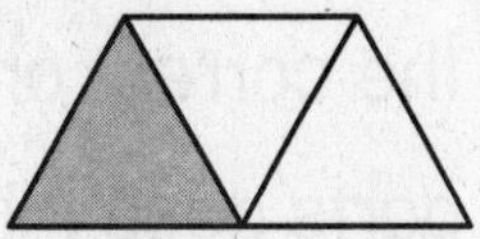

$\frac{1}{3}$	$\frac{1}{2}$	$\frac{1}{4}$	NH
○	○	○	○

Use with text pages 229–230.

Name ______________________ Date ____________

Practice 9.2

Other Fractions

Write the fraction for the shaded parts.

Remember
The fraction names part of a whole.

1. two shaded parts

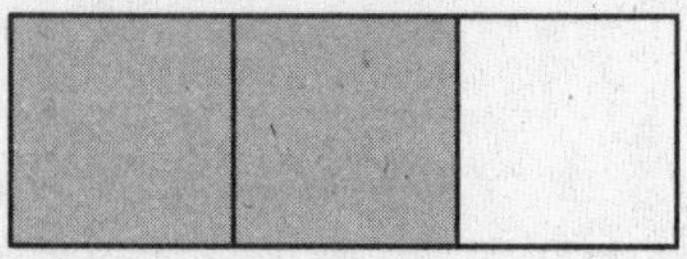

$\frac{2}{3}$

2. one shaded part

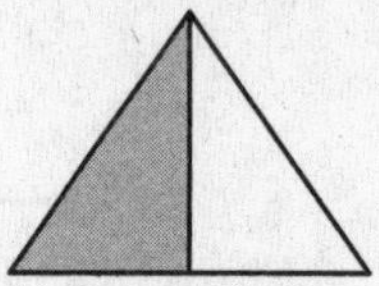

____

3. four shaded parts

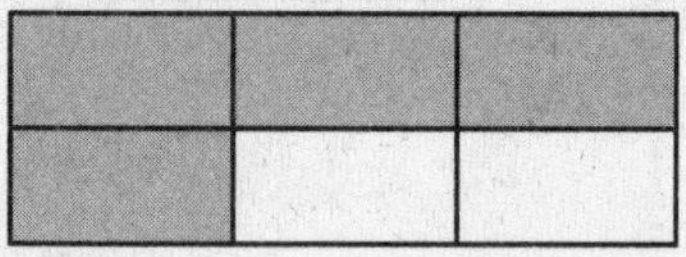

____

4. eight shaded parts

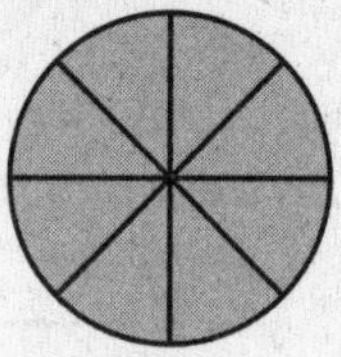

____

Color to show the number of shaded parts.
Write the fraction for the shaded parts.

5. three shaded parts

____

6. six shaded parts

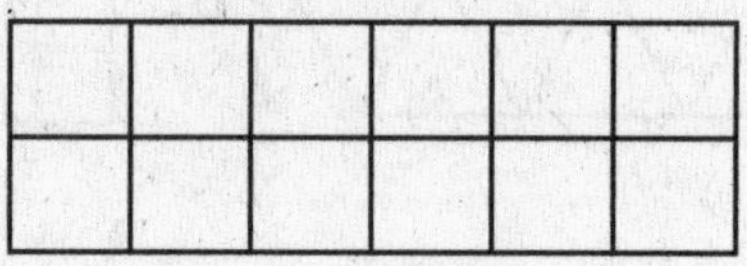

____

7. four shaded parts

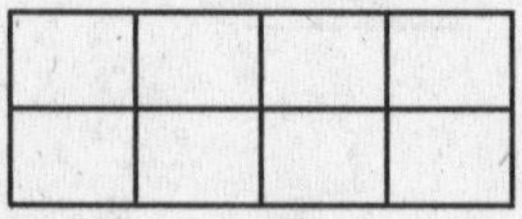

____

8. three shaded parts

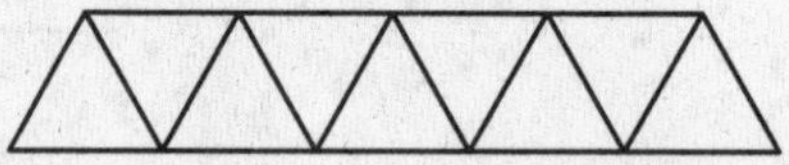

____

Test Prep

Fill in the ○ for the correct answer. NH means Not Here.

9. How many parts does this shape show?

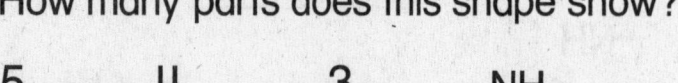

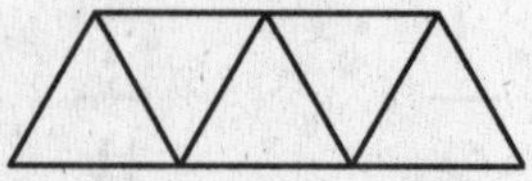

5	4	3	NH
○	○	○	○

Use with text pages 231–232.

Name ______________________ Date ______________

Comparing Fractions

Compare the shaded parts.
Write > or < to compare fractions.

Remember
> is greater than
and
< is less than.

1.

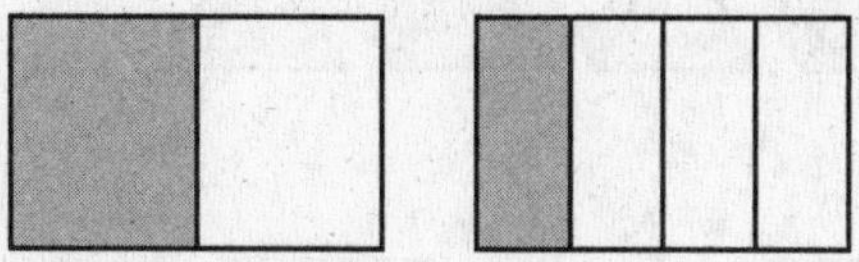

$\frac{1}{2}$ ○ $\frac{1}{4}$

2.

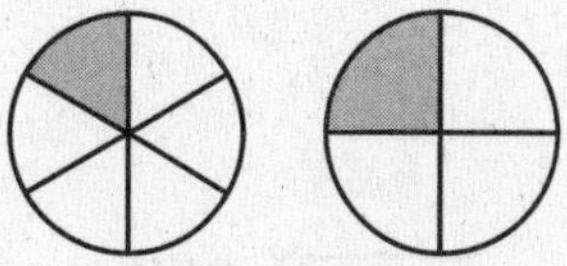

$\frac{1}{6}$ ○ $\frac{1}{4}$

3.

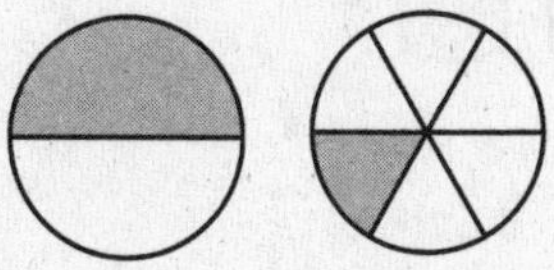

$\frac{1}{2}$ ○ $\frac{1}{6}$

4.

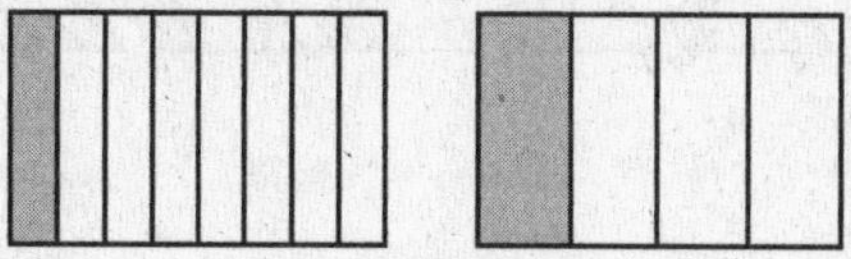

$\frac{1}{8}$ ○ $\frac{1}{4}$

5.

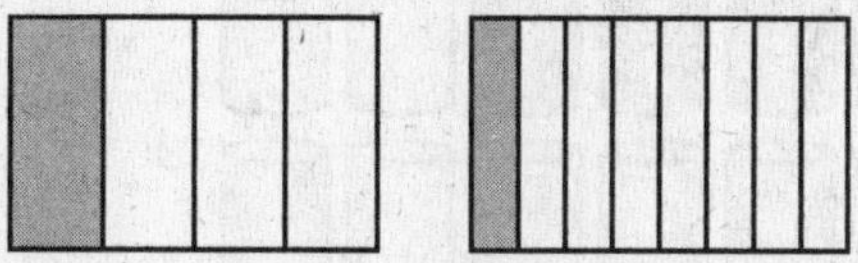

$\frac{1}{4}$ ○ $\frac{1}{8}$

6.

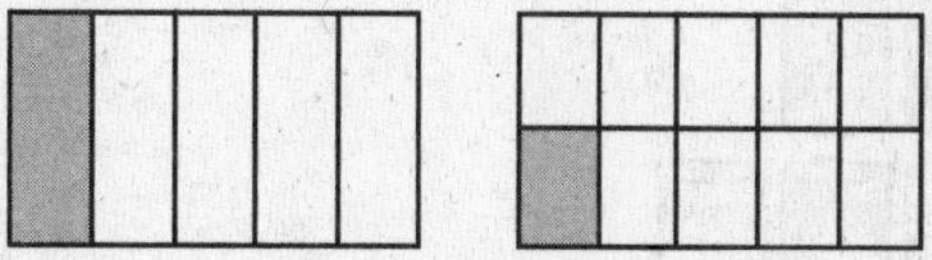

$\frac{1}{5}$ ○ $\frac{1}{10}$

Test Prep

Fill in the ○ for the correct answer. NH means Not Here.

7. Compare. Choose the symbol.

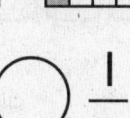

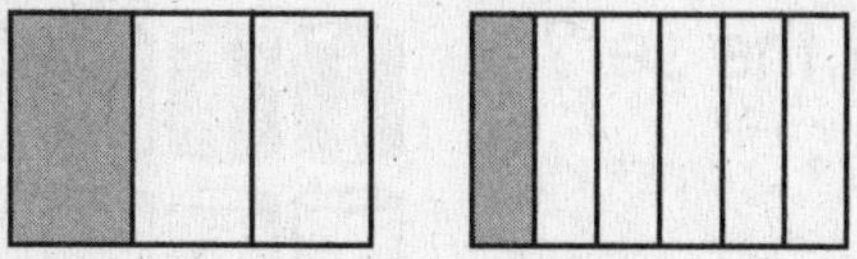

$\frac{1}{3}$ ○ $\frac{1}{6}$

>	<	=	NH
○	○	○	○

Use with text pages 235–236.

Name ______________________ Date ____________

Fractions of a Set

Write a fraction for each color.

1.

$\frac{3}{6}$ black $\frac{3}{6}$ gray

2.

____ black ____ gray

3.

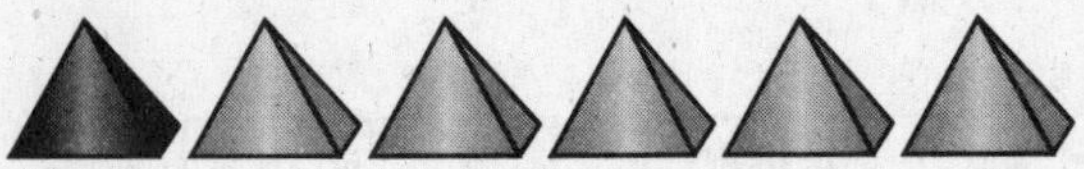

____ black ____ gray

4.

____ black ____ gray

5.

____ black ____ gray

6.

____ black ____ gray

Test Prep

Fill in the ○ for the correct answer. NH means Not Here.

7. What fraction names the black parts of the set?

$\frac{2}{8}$ ○ $\frac{3}{8}$ ○ $\frac{4}{8}$ ○ NH ○

Use with text pages 237–238.

Name ______________________ Date ____________

Practice 9.5

Problem Solving: Use a Picture

Use the picture. Color to solve the problem.

1. Max has 6 soccer cards. He gives 4 to Rosie. What fraction of the cards does Max give to Rosie?

$\frac{4}{6}$ of the cards

2. Patsy has 4 shells. She gives 1 shell to Lewis. What fraction of the shells does Patsy have left?

____ of the shells

3. Benjamin brings 12 oranges to baseball practice. The team eats 6 oranges. What fraction of oranges does the team eat?

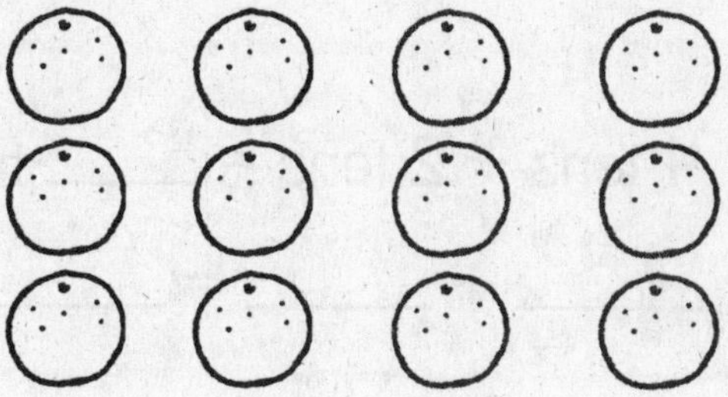

____ of the oranges

Test Prep

Fill in the ○ for the correct answer. NH means Not Here.

4. Use the picture. Solve.

Mrs. Wells cut an apple pie into 8 pieces. The children eat 6 pieces. What fraction of the pie is left?

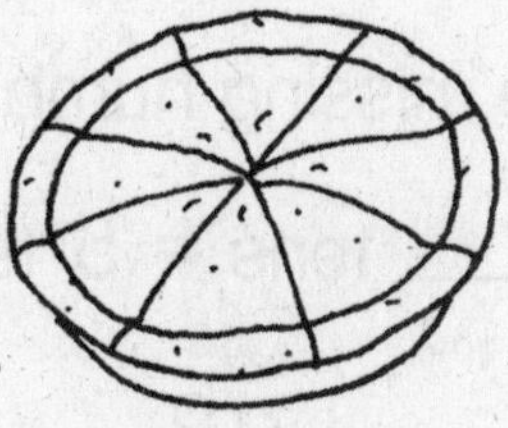

$\frac{6}{8}$	$\frac{4}{8}$	$\frac{2}{8}$	NH
○	○	○	○

Use with text pages 239–241.

Name ______________________ Date ____________

Practice 10.1

Mental Math: Add Tens

Remember
Think about addition facts.

Complete the addition sentences. Use a basic fact to help.

1. 2 tens + 6 tens = 8 tens
20 + 60 = 80

2. 5 tens + 3 tens = _____ tens
_____ + _____ = _____

3. 3 tens + 4 tens = _____ tens
_____ + _____ = _____

4. 1 ten + 1 ten = _____ tens
_____ + _____ = _____

5. 7 tens + 1 ten = _____ tens
_____ + _____ = _____

6. 3 tens + 6 tens = _____ tens
_____ + _____ = _____

7. 4 tens + 2 tens = _____ tens
_____ + _____ = _____

8. 1 ten + 8 tens = _____ tens
_____ + _____ = _____

9. 2 tens + 7 tens = _____ tens
_____ + _____ = _____

10. 2 tens + 2 tens = _____ tens
_____ + _____ = _____

Test Prep

Fill in the ○ for the correct answer. NH means Not Here.

11. What is the missing number?

1 ten + _____ tens = 5 tens

4	3	2	NH
○	○	○	○

Use with text pages 263–264.

Practice
10.2

Count on Tens to Add

Use the hundred chart.
Add.

1. $27 + 30 =$ __57__

2. $10 + 16 =$ _____

3. $43 + 30 =$ _____

4. $50 + 21 =$ _____

5. $82 + 10 =$ _____

6. $60 + 25 =$ _____

1	2	3	4	5	6	7	8	9	10
11	12	13	14	15	16	17	18	19	20
21	22	23	24	25	26	27	28	29	30
31	32	33	34	35	36	37	38	39	40
41	42	43	44	45	46	47	48	49	50
51	52	53	54	55	56	57	58	59	60
61	62	63	64	65	66	67	68	69	70
71	72	73	74	75	76	77	78	79	80
81	82	83	84	85	86	87	88	89	90
91	92	93	94	95	96	97	98	99	100

7. $\begin{array}{r} 11 \\ + 40 \\ \hline \end{array}$ 8. $\begin{array}{r} 20 \\ + 32 \\ \hline \end{array}$ 9. $\begin{array}{r} 79 \\ + 10 \\ \hline \end{array}$ 10. $\begin{array}{r} 50 \\ + 14 \\ \hline \end{array}$

11. $\begin{array}{r} 10 \\ + 57 \\ \hline \end{array}$ 12. $\begin{array}{r} 40 \\ + 51 \\ \hline \end{array}$ 13. $\begin{array}{r} 62 \\ + 10 \\ \hline \end{array}$ 14. $\begin{array}{r} 30 \\ + 31 \\ \hline \end{array}$

Test Prep

Fill in the ○ for the correct answer. NH means Not Here.

15. What is the missing number?

$17 +$ ____ $= 47$

20 40 60 NH
○ ○ ○ ○

Use with text pages 265–266.

Name ______________________ Date ____________

Practice 10.3

Regroup Ones as Tens

Use Workmat 3 with [ten block] and [one block].
Write the tens and ones.
Regroup. Write the number.

Remember
Regroup
10 ones as 1 ten.

1. 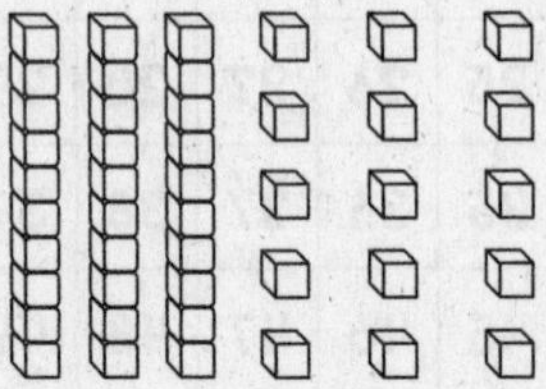 **Regroup** → 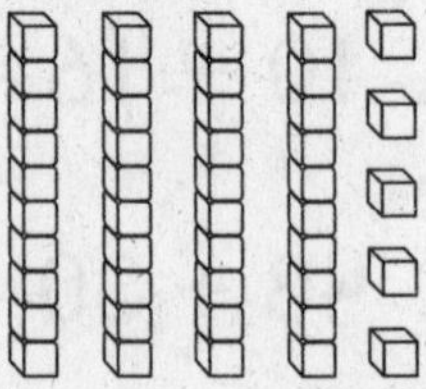

3 tens 15 ones → 4 tens 5 ones [45]

Regroup. Write the number.

2. 6 tens 10 ones **Regroup** → ____ tens ____ ones [ ]

3. 5 tens 14 ones **Regroup** → ____ tens ____ ones [ ]

4. 1 ten 19 ones **Regroup** → ____ tens ____ ones [ ]

5. 7 tens 13 ones **Regroup** → ____ tens ____ ones [ ]

6. 2 tens 11 ones **Regroup** → ____ tens ____ one [ ]

Test Prep

Fill in the ○ for the correct answer. NH means Not Here.

7. How many tens are there after you regroup 2 tens and 18 ones?

3	2	1	NH
○	○	○	○

Use with text pages 267–269.

Name ______________________ Date ______________

Practice 11.3

Choose a Way to Add

Choose a way to add. Add.
Explain the way you find the sum.

1. 42 + 20

   62; Explanations may vary. I used mental math. I just counted 52, 62.

2. 50 + 7

3. 39 + 26

4. 84 + 10

5. 40 + 9

6. 68 + 17 =

Test Prep

7. Fill in the ○ for the correct answer. NH means Not Here.
   Find the sum.

   35 + 30

45	55	65	NH
○	○	○	○

Use with text pages 293–294.

Name ______________________ Date ______________

Add Three Numbers

Remember
Look for a ten or a double.

Add.

1. 15 + 20 + 15 = 50

2. 13 + 50 + 17

3. 3 + 17 + 21

4. 13 + 33 + 41

5. 2 + 38 + 22

6. 44 + 16 + 5

7. 63 + 21 + 3

8. 58 + 21 + 12

9. 27 + 17 + 10

10. 8 + 18 + 22

11. 33 + 22 + 13

12. 22 + 30 + 8

Test Prep

13. Will finding a ten or finding a double help you solve this problem? What numbers in the ones column will help you? Write your answers.

56 + 14 + 22

____

____

____

Use with text pages 297–298.

Name ______________________ Date ____________

Practice 11.5

Problem Solving: Guess and Check

Use Guess and Check to solve.

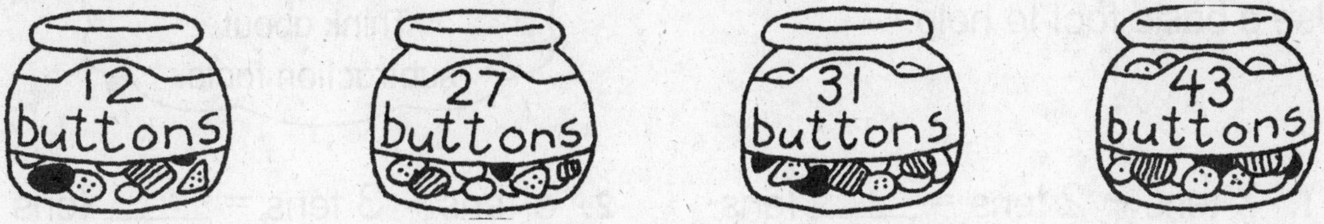

Draw or write to explain.

1. Mrs. Tucker needs 55 buttons for some button dolls that she is making. Which jars should she buy?

   12 and 43

2. The button store sold 58 buttons to the High Street Elementary School. Which two jars of buttons did the school buy?

   ______ and ______

3. Mr. Richards needs 70 buttons for an art project. Which two jars of buttons should Mr. Richards buy?

   ______ and ______

Test Prep

Fill in the ○ for the correct answer. NH means Not Here.

4. Guess and check to solve.

   Zeke bought 50 toy animals for a party. Which two jars of animals did Zeke buy?

22 + 16	22 + 34	34 + 16	NH
○	○	○	○

Use with text pages 299–301.

Name ______________________ Date ____________

Mental Math: Subtract Tens

Complete the subtraction sentences.
Use a basic fact to help.

Remember
Think about subtraction facts.

1. 7 tens − 2 tens = 5 tens

   70 − 20 = 50

2. 6 tens − 3 tens = ____ tens

   ____ − ____ = ____

3. 9 tens − 5 tens = ____ tens

   ____ − ____ = ____

4. 4 tens − 1 ten = ____ tens

   ____ − ____ = ____

5. 8 tens − 6 tens = ____ tens

   ____ − ____ = ____

6. 9 tens − 2 tens = ____ tens

   ____ − ____ = ____

7. 5 tens − 3 tens = ____ tens

   ____ − ____ = ____

8. 7 tens − 4 tens = ____ tens

   ____ − ____ = ____

9. 6 tens − 2 tens = ____ tens

   ____ − ____ = ____

10. 8 tens − 2 tens = ____ tens

    ____ − ____ = ____

Test Prep

11. Write the missing number.

    9 tens − 6 tens = 3 tens

    ____ − 60 = 30

Use with text pages 323–324.

Name ______________________ Date ____________

Practice 12.2

Subtract Tens on a Hundred Chart

Use the hundred chart.
Subtract.

Remember
Move up 1 row for each ten you subtract.

1. 53 − 20 = 33

2. 78 − 30 = ____

3. 62 − 10 = ____

4. 85 − 30 = ____

5. 49 − 30 = ____

6. 74 − 20 = ____

1	2	3	4	5	6	7	8	9	10
11	12	13	14	15	16	17	18	19	20
21	22	23	24	25	26	27	28	29	30
31	32	33	34	35	36	37	38	39	40
41	42	43	44	45	46	47	48	49	50
51	52	53	54	55	56	57	58	59	60
61	62	63	64	65	66	67	68	69	70
71	72	73	74	75	76	77	78	79	80
81	82	83	84	85	86	87	88	89	90
91	92	93	94	95	96	97	98	99	100

7. 57 − 30

8. 90 − 40

9. 74 − 10

10. 61 − 20

11. 82 − 40

12. 52 − 10

13. 68 − 50

14. 87 − 40

Test Prep

Fill in the ○ for the correct answer.

15. Which number completes the sentence? ____ − 30 = 18

○ 48 ○ 50 ○ 56 ○ 58

Use with text pages 325–326.

Name ______________________ Date ______________

Regroup Tens

Use Workmat 3 with [ten rod] and [cube].
Regroup 1 ten. Write the tens and ones.

Remember
Regroup 1 ten as 10 ones.

1. 73	7 tens 3 ones	Regroup	6 tens 13 ones
2. 57	5 tens 7 ones	Regroup	___ tens ___ ones
3. 65	6 tens 5 ones	Regroup	___ tens ___ ones
4. 86	8 tens 6 ones	Regroup	___ tens ___ ones
5. 49	4 tens 9 ones	Regroup	___ tens ___ ones
6. 54	5 tens 4 ones	Regroup	___ tens ___ ones
7. 92	9 tens 2 ones	Regroup	___ tens ___ ones
8. 70	7 tens 0 ones	Regroup	___ tens ___ ones
9. 34	3 tens 4 ones	Regroup	___ tens ___ ones
10. 81	8 tens 1 one	Regroup	___ tens ___ ones

Test Prep

Fill in the ○ for the correct answer. NH means Not Here.

11. Regroup 1 ten and 1 one.
How many ones are there now?

11	10	5	NH
○	○	○	○

Use with text pages 327–328.

Name ______________________ Date ____________

Practice 12.4

Decide When to Regroup

Use Workmat 3 with and .

Show the greater number.	Do you need to regroup to subtract?	Subtract the ones. How many tens and ones are left?	What is the difference?
1. 45 − 9	Yes (circled) No	3 tens 6 ones	36
2. 68 − 3	Yes No	____ tens ____ ones	
3. 72 − 5	Yes No	____ tens ____ ones	
4. 58 − 8	Yes No	____ tens ____ ones	
5. 92 − 4	Yes No	____ tens ____ ones	
6. 36 − 9	Yes No	____ tens ____ ones	
7. 29 − 7	Yes No	____ tens ____ ones	
8. 81 − 5	Yes No	____ tens ____ ones	

Test Prep

9. Write a subtraction sentence that needs regrouping.

Use with text pages 329–330.

Name ______________________ Date __________

Practice 12.5

Subtract One-Digit Numbers From Two-Digit Numbers

Use Workmat 3 with tens and ones. Subtract.

1.

	Tens	Ones
	5	13
	~~6~~	~~3~~
−		8
	5	5

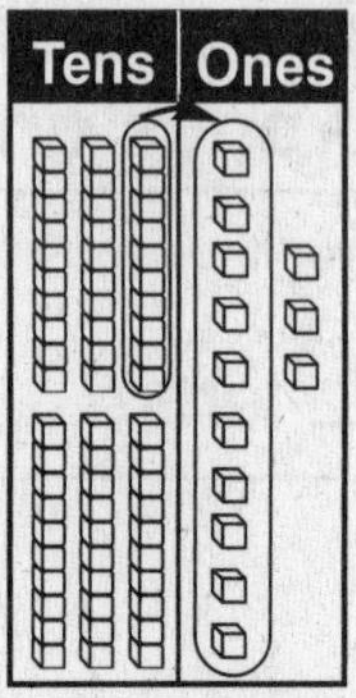

2.

	Tens	Ones
	4	5
−		6

3.

	Tens	Ones
	5	7
−		4

4.

	Tens	Ones
	7	2
−		6

5.

	Tens	Ones
	8	4
−		9

6.

	Tens	Ones
	3	6
−		8

7.

	Tens	Ones
	4	1
−		4

8.

	Tens	Ones
	5	8
−		7

9.

	Tens	Ones
	9	3
−		5

10.

	Tens	Ones
	6	7
−		8

11.

	Tens	Ones
	7	0
−		6

Test Prep

Fill in the ○ for the correct answer. NH means Not Here.

12. When you subtract 73 − 9, how many ones are in the difference?

0	2	4	NH
○	○	○	○

Use with text pages 333–334.

Name ____________________ Date ____________

Practice 12.6

Subtract Two-Digit Numbers

Use Workmat 3 with [ten rod] and [unit cube]. Subtract.

> **Remember**
> Record the number of tens and ones when you regroup.

1.

	Tens	Ones
	4	16
	~~5~~	~~6~~
−	2	7
	2	9

2.

	Tens	Ones
	3	4
−	1	6

3.

	Tens	Ones
	7	5
−	3	8

4.

	Tens	Ones
	6	1
−	4	5

5.

	Tens	Ones
	4	8
−	1	5

6.

	Tens	Ones
	7	4
−	3	1

7.

	Tens	Ones
	8	5
−	3	8

8.

	Tens	Ones
	6	3
−	1	7

9.

	Tens	Ones
	7	0
−	4	5

10.

	Tens	Ones
	9	5
−	2	9

11.

	Tens	Ones
	6	3
−	4	3

Test Prep

Fill in the ○ for the correct answer. NH means Not Here.

12. When this number is subtracted from 85, it gives you a difference with a 0 in the ones place. What is the number?

15	20	30	NH
○	○	○	○

Use with text pages 335–336.

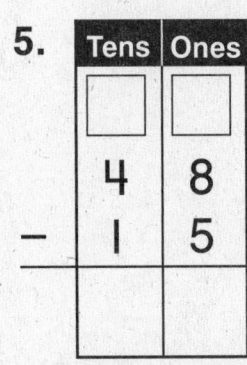

Name ______________________ Date ____________

Problem Solving: Use a Table

Use the table to solve the problems.

School Fair Food Sales

Foods	Number Sold
Hot Dogs	35
Veggie Burgers	67
Rice and Beans	19
Salads	48

1. The food booth sells food at the school fair. How many more hot dogs were sold than plates of rice and beans?

   Think
   Do I add or subtract?

   16 more hot dogs

2. How many rice and beans and salads were sold in all?

   _____ in all

3. How many more veggie burgers were sold than salads?

   _____ more veggie burgers

Draw or write to explain.

Test Prep

Fill in the ○ for the correct answer.

4. At the fair, 16 children buy juice. 45 children buy milk. How many more children buy milk than buy juice?

   61 ○   51 ○   31 ○   29 ○

Use with text pages 337–339.

Name ______________________ Date ______________

Practice 13.1

Rewrite to Subtract

Write the numbers in vertical form. Subtract.

Remember
Line up the ones and the tens.

1. 37 − 19

Tens	Ones
2	17
3	7
− 1	9
1	8

2. 54 − 21

Tens	Ones
−	

3. 66 − 37

Tens	Ones
−	

4. 98 − 16

Tens	Ones
−	

5. 50 − 25

Tens	Ones
−	

6. 86 − 59

Tens	Ones
−	

7. 75 − 20

Tens	Ones
−	

8. 41 − 3

Tens	Ones
−	

Test Prep

Fill in the ○ for the correct answer.

9. Write the numbers in vertical form. Subtract.

75 − 36

41 ○ 40 ○ 39 ○ 35 ○

Tens	Ones
−	

Use with text pages 347–348.

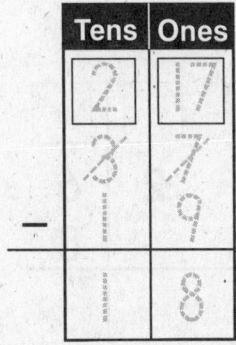

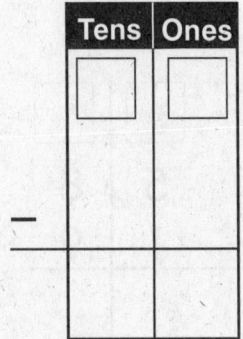

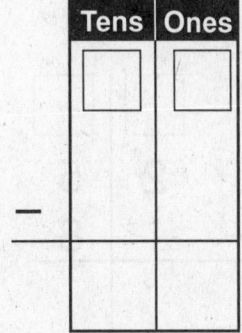

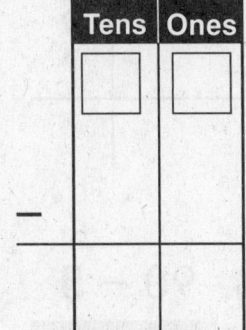

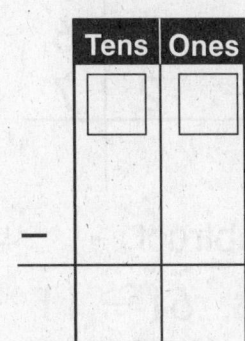

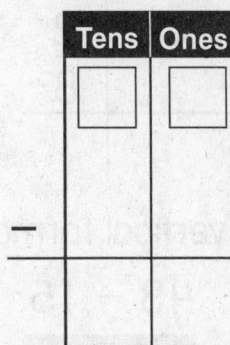

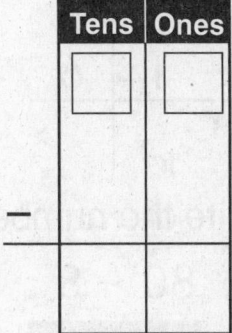

Name ______________________ Date ____________

Practice 13.2

More Two-Digit Subtraction

Subtract.

1.
7	12
8	2
− 3	4
4	8

2.
4	4
− 2	1

3.
9	3
− 6	8

4.
6	5
− 3	5

5.
3	6
−	5

6.
2	5
− 1	8

7.
5	8
− 1	9

8.
2	6
−	8

9.
7	6
− 1	6

10.
3	2
−	8

11.
5	6
− 2	7

12.
5	5
− 1	1

Write the numbers in vertical format. Subtract.

13. 80 − 8

Tens	Ones
−	

14. 43 − 15

Tens	Ones
−	

15. 61 − 11

Tens	Ones
−	

16. 90 − 5

Tens	Ones
−	

Test Prep

17. Fill in the ○ for the correct answer.

45 − 29

26	17	16	15
○	○	○	○

Use with text pages 349–350.

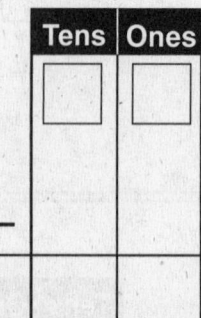

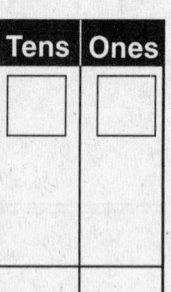

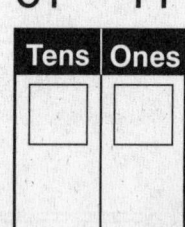

Name ______________________ Date ______________

Practice 13.3

Estimate Differences

Round each number to the nearest ten.
Estimate the difference.

> **Remember**
> Round up if the number has five ones or more.

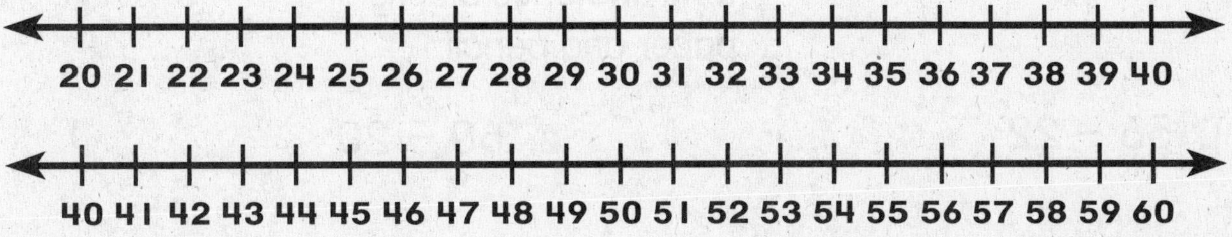

1. 46 − 22

   50 − 20 = 30

2. 55 − 28

   ____ − ____ = ____

3. 44 − 31

   ____ − ____ = ____

4. 56 − 26

   ____ − ____ = ____

5. 45 − 22

   ____ − ____ = ____

6. 38 − 36

   ____ − ____ = ____

7. 43 − 29

   ____ − ____ = ____

8. 49 − 21

   ____ − ____ = ____

Test Prep

Fill in the ○ for the correct answer. NH means Not Here.

9. Estimate the difference.

   56 − 22

30	40	50	NH
○	○	○	○

Use with text pages 351–352.

Name ______________________ Date ____________

Practice 13.4

Choose a Way to Subtract

Choose a way to subtract.

Explain how you find the difference.

Different ways to subtract:
- mental math
- calculator
- tens and ones blocks
- paper and pencil

1. 56 − 22

34; Possible response: I used paper and pencil so I could line up the tens and ones in the two numbers.

2. 60 − 20

3. 64 − 17

4. 94 − 56

Test Prep

5. Write a subtraction sentence that someone could solve easily with mental math.

Use with text pages 355–356.

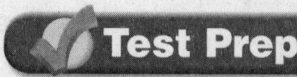

Use Addition to Check Subtraction

Subtract. Check by adding.

1. $\begin{array}{r} 87 \\ -\ 68 \\ \hline 19 \end{array}$ $\begin{array}{r} \boxed{19} \\ +\ \boxed{68} \\ \hline \boxed{87} \end{array}$

2. $\begin{array}{r} 95 \\ -\ 10 \\ \hline \end{array}$ $\begin{array}{r} \boxed{} \\ +\ \boxed{} \\ \hline \boxed{} \end{array}$

3. $\begin{array}{r} 75 \\ -\ 58 \\ \hline \end{array}$ $\begin{array}{r} \boxed{} \\ +\ \boxed{} \\ \hline \boxed{} \end{array}$

4. $\begin{array}{r} 63 \\ -\ 5 \\ \hline \end{array}$ $\begin{array}{r} \boxed{} \\ +\ \boxed{} \\ \hline \boxed{} \end{array}$

5. $\begin{array}{r} 52 \\ -\ 10 \\ \hline \end{array}$ $\begin{array}{r} \boxed{} \\ +\ \boxed{} \\ \hline \boxed{} \end{array}$

6. $\begin{array}{r} 25 \\ -\ 6 \\ \hline \end{array}$ $\begin{array}{r} \boxed{} \\ +\ \boxed{} \\ \hline \boxed{} \end{array}$

7. $\begin{array}{r} 76 \\ -\ 12 \\ \hline \end{array}$ $\begin{array}{r} \boxed{} \\ +\ \boxed{} \\ \hline \boxed{} \end{array}$

8. $\begin{array}{r} 35 \\ -\ 5 \\ \hline \end{array}$ $\begin{array}{r} \boxed{} \\ +\ \boxed{} \\ \hline \boxed{} \end{array}$

Test Prep

Fill in the ○ for the correct answer. NH means Not Here.

9. Subtract.

$52 - 26$

36 26 25 NH
○ ○ ○ ○

Use with text pages 357–358.

Name ______________________ Date ______________

Practice 13.6

Choose the Operation

Find the parts and whole to solve. Write the answer.

Draw or write to explain.

1. There are 52 children on two soccer teams. 27 children are on Team A. How many children are on Team B?

Whole	
25	
Part	**Part**
52	27

25 children

2. The second graders invite 22 third graders and 20 first graders to their class play. How many children do they invite?

Whole	
Part	**Part**

______ children

3. The art class drew 46 animal postcards and 35 flower postcards. How many postcards did they draw in all?

Whole	
Part	**Part**

______ postcards

4. The science class collected 22 sea shells and 10 pieces of sea glass. How many more sea shells than sea glass did they collect?

Whole	
Part	**Part**

______ sea shells

Test Prep

5. Write which math operation you would use to solve.

The children blew up 25 yellow balloons and 36 green balloons for the party. How many balloons did they blow up? ______________

Use with text pages 359–361.

Name ______________________ Date ____________

Practice 14.1

Pennies, Nickels, and Dimes

Remember
Count on by 10s, 5s, and 1s.

Count on to find the value of the coins.

1.

10 ¢ 20 ¢ 25 ¢ 30 ¢ 30 ¢ total

2.

_____¢ _____¢ _____¢ _____¢ _____¢ total

3.

_____¢ _____¢ _____¢ _____¢ _____¢ total

4.

_____¢ _____¢ _____¢ _____¢ _____¢ total

Test Prep

Fill in the ○ for the correct answer. NH means Not Here.

5. Count on to find the value of the coins.

37¢	27¢	25¢	NH
○	○	○	○

Use with text pages 383–384.

Name ______________________ Date ____________

Practice 14.2

Quarters and Half-Dollars

Count on to find the value of the coins.

1. 

_____¢ _____¢ _____¢

2. 

_____¢ _____¢ _____¢

3. 

_____¢ _____¢ _____¢

4. 

_____¢ _____¢ _____¢

Test Prep

Fill in the ○ for the correct answer.

5. Count on to find the value of the coins.

60¢ ○ 50¢ ○ 51¢ ○ 26¢ ○

Use with text pages 385–386.

Name ____________________ Date __________

Count Coins

Use coins.
Count on to find the value of the coins.

Remember
Start counting with the coin of the greatest value.

1.

_____¢

2.

_____¢

3.

_____¢

4.

_____¢

5.

_____¢

6.

_____¢

Test Prep

5. Circle the name.
Who has more money?

Josh

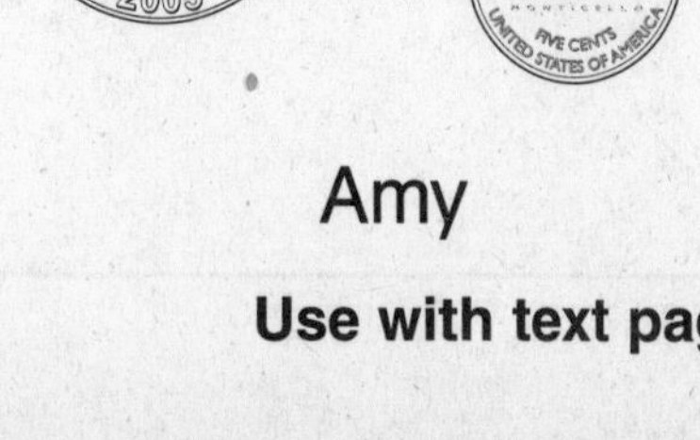

Amy

Use with text pages 387–389.

Name ____________________ Date ____________

One Dollar

Write the value of the coins.
Circle the groups of coins that equal one dollar.

1. 

$1.00

2. 

____

3. 

____

4. 

____

Find the value of the coins. Circle the correct answer.

5. 

less than $1.00

equal to $1.00

Test Prep

6. Draw dimes to equal one dollar.

Use with text pages 391–393.

Name ______________________ Date ____________

Practice 14.5

Equal Amounts

Use coins.
Show two ways
to make each amount.
Draw the coins.

Remember Draw the coins like this.

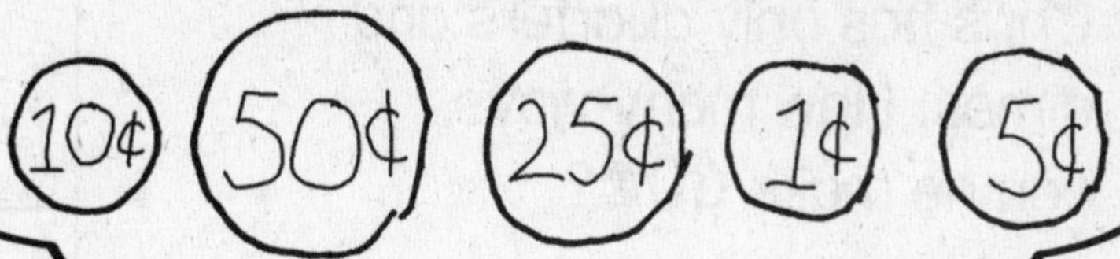

1. 56¢

2. 56¢

3. 82¢

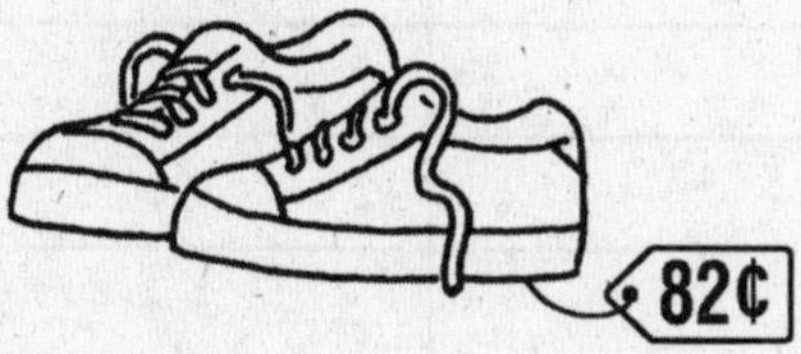

4. 82¢

5. 95¢

6. 95¢

Test Prep

7. Draw more coins to make the amount 76¢.

Use with text pages 395–396.

Name ______________________ Date ____________

Make a List

Use coins to solve. Complete the list.

Draw or write to explain.

1. Chris has only quarters and dimes. How many ways can he make 60¢?

2 ways

25¢	10¢
2	1
	6

2. Jan wants a toy yo-yo for 45¢. She has quarters, dimes, and nickels. How many ways can she make 45¢?

_____ ways

25¢	10¢	5¢

3. Mick has only dimes and nickels. How many ways can he make 20¢?

_____ ways

10¢	5¢

Test Prep

Fill in the ○ for the correct answer. NH means Not Here.

4. Rick makes 50¢ with dimes and nickels. If he uses 3 dimes, how many nickels does he use?

6	4	3	NH
○	○	○	○

Use with text pages 397–399.

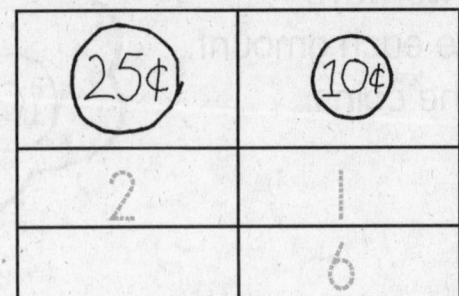

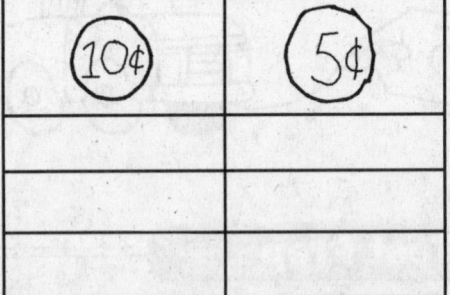

Name ______________________ Date ______________

Practice 15.1

Make an Exact Amount

Circle the coins that make the exact amount.

1.

2.

3.

Test Prep

Fill in the ○ for the correct answer. NH means Not Here.

4. What amount do these coins show?

48¢ ○   56¢ ○   60¢ ○   NH ○

Use with text pages 407–408.

Name ______________________ Date ____________

Practice 15.2

Compare Money Values

Write the value of the set of coins. Compare the sets.

1. 

40 ¢ (>)  37 ¢

2. 

_____ ¢ ( )  _____ ¢

3. 

_____ ¢ ( )  _____ ¢

4. 

_____ ¢ ( )  _____ ¢

Test Prep

5. Circle the answer.
How does Set 1 compare with Set 2?

Set 1 is _____ Set 2.

less than greater than equal to

Set 1

Set 2

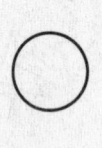

Use with text pages 409–410.

Name ______________________ Date ____________

Practice 15.3

Use the Fewest Coins

Remember
Start with the coin of the greatest value.

Find the fewest coins that show the amount. Draw the coins.

1.

2.

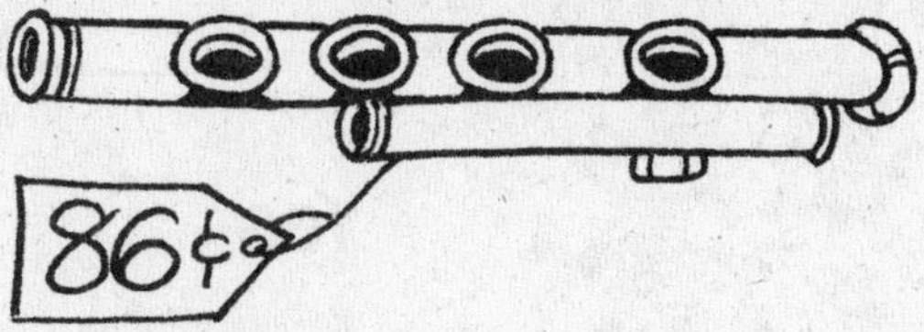

3.

4.

Test Prep

Fill in the ○ for the correct answer.

5. Which coin would you start counting with to make 98¢?

○

○

○

○

Use with text pages 411–412.

Name ______________________ Date ____________

Compare Prices and Amounts

Write the amount of money.
Is there enough? Circle **Yes** or **No**.

1.

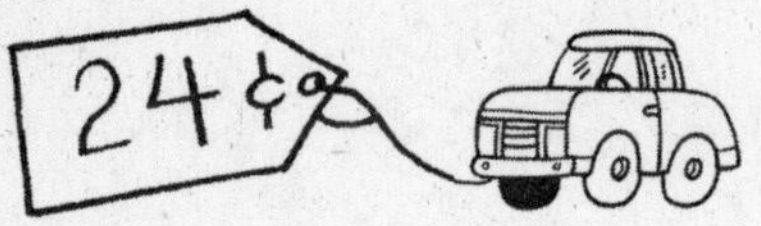

25 ¢

Yes No

2.

_____¢

Yes No

3.

_____¢

Yes No

Test Prep

Fill in the ○ for the correct answer. NH means Not Here.

4. Which coin do you need to buy the  ?

NH

○ ○ ○ ○

Use with text pages 413–414.

Name ______________________ Date ____________

Practice 15.5

Add and Subtract Amounts of Money

Add or subtract.

Remember
Write the ¢ in your answer

1. 87¢ − 19¢ = 68¢ (7 17 regrouping shown)

2. 45¢ + 20¢

3. 24¢ + 18¢

4. 99¢ − 9¢

5. 60¢ + 15¢

6. 80¢ − 10¢

7. 59¢ − 15¢

8

Rewrite the numbers. Then add or subtract.

9. 62¢ − 17¢

10. 49¢ − 26¢

11. 33¢ + 17¢

12. 27¢ + 9¢

Test Prep

Circle the answer.

13. What is another way to write the numbers?

50¢
−29¢

29¢ − 50¢ 50¢ − 29¢ 29¢ + 50¢

Use with text pages 417–418.

Name ______________________ Date ______________

Practice 15.6

Make Change With Pennies and Nickels

Write the amount paid. Draw the coins and count on to find the change.

Amount Paid	Price	Draw Coins to Count On	Change
1.  30¢	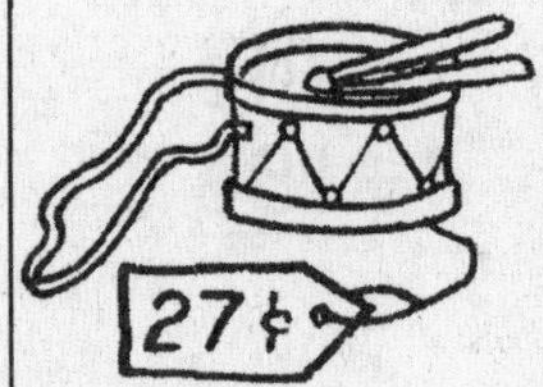	28¢ 29¢ 30¢	3¢
2.  ____ ¢		____ ¢ ____ ¢	____ ¢
3.  ____ ¢	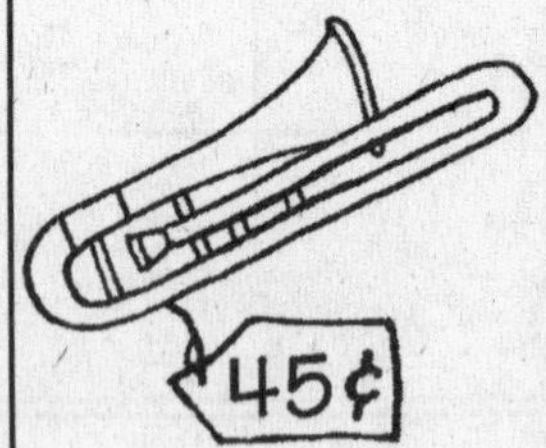	____ ¢	____ ¢

Test Prep

Fill in the ○ for the correct answer.

4. I paid 78¢. It costs 73¢. What is my change?

15¢	10¢	5¢	No Change
○	○	○	○

Use with text pages 419–420.

Name ______________________ Date ____________

Practice 15.7

Make Change with Nickels, Dimes, and Quarters

Write the amount paid. Draw the coins and count on to find the change.

Amount Paid	Price	Draw Coins to Count On	Change
1.  75¢		70¢ 75¢	15¢
2.  ______		______	______
3.  ______		______ ______	______

Test Prep

Fill in the ○ for the correct answer. NH means Not Here.

4. Which is the correct change?

	20¢	25¢	$1.00	NH
Milo pays 65¢. He buys a little book for 45¢.	○	○	○	○

Use with text pages 421–422.

Name ______________________ Date ____________

Problem Solving: Act It Out With Models

Use coins to act out the problem. Solve.

1. Lucy has 50¢. Then she earns 25¢ watering the plants for her grandmother. How much money does she have now? 75¢	Draw or write to explain.
2. Juan has 3 dimes and 1 nickel. How much more money does he need to buy a muffin for 45¢? ____	
3. Bettina has 20¢. How much more money does she need to buy a flower charm for 50¢? ____	

Test Prep

4. Write the answer.
Draw coins if you wish.

Tommy has 2 quarters and 2 nickels. How much more money does he need to buy a toy for 75¢?

____

Use with text pages 423–425.

Name ______________________ Date ____________

Activity: Estimate Time

about 1 hour

It takes about 1 second to touch your toes.
It takes about 1 minute to put on your socks.
It takes about 1 hour to play a board game.

Think about the length of time.
Draw or write things you do that take that long.

1. About 10 seconds
2. About 5 minutes
3. About 1 hour

Test Prep

Circle the answer.

4. How much time would it take to eat lunch?

seconds   minutes

Use with text pages 433–434.

Name ______________________ Date ____________

Practice 16.2

Time to the Hour and Half-Hour

Remember
The minute hand points to 12 at the hour. The minute hand points to 6 at the half-hour.

Write the time.

1.

7:30

2.

___ : ___

3.

___ : ___

4.

___ : ___

Draw the minute hand to show the time.

5.

5:00

6.

8:30

7.

11:00

8.

2:30

Test Prep

9. Draw a clock.
Then show 4:30.

Use with text pages 435–436.

Name ______________________ Date ____________

Practice 16.3

Time to Five Minutes

Write the time.

1. 
3:50

2. 
___:___

3. 
___:___

4. 
___:___

5. 
___:___

6. 
___:___

7. 
___:___

8. 
___:___

Draw the minute hand to show the time.

9. 

10. 

11. 

12. 

Test Prep

13. The times show a pattern. Write the time that comes next.

7:50 7:55 8:00 8:05 ________

Use with text pages 437–438.

Name ____________________ Date __________

Time to 15 Minutes

Write the time.

1.  6:15	2.  ___:___	3.  ___:___	4.  ___:___
5.  ___:___	6.  ___:___	7.  ___:___	8.  ___:___

Draw the minute hand to show the time.

9.  12:15	10.  3:00	11.  8:45	12.  11:30

Test Prep

Fill in the ○ for the correct answer.

13. What time does the clock show?

7:50	7:55	8:00	6:45
○	○	○	○

Use with text pages 441–442.

Name ____________________ Date ____________

Practice 16.5

Elapsed Time

Write the times. Then write how much time has passed.

On Sale	Start Time	End Time	How long does the sale last?
1. 	 2:00 P.M.	 4:00 P.M.	2 hours
2. 	 ___:___ A.M.	 ___:___ A.M.	___ hours
3. 	 ___:___ P.M.	 ___:___ P.M.	___ hours

Test Prep

Draw hands on the clock to show that 2 hours have passed.

Use with text pages 445–446.

Name ______________________ Date ____________

Practice 16.6

Use a Calendar

This calendar shows 1 year.
Use the calendar to answer the questions.

1. What is the date one week after May 1? May 8

2. How many months are in one year? ______ months

3. What is the ninth month of the year? ____________

4. What date follows March 31? ____________

5. Which months have 31 days?

____

____

____

____

January 2009

S	M	T	W	T	F	S
				1	2	3
4	5	6	7	8	9	10
11	12	13	14	15	16	17
18	19	20	21	22	23	24
25	26	27	28	29	30	31

February 2009

S	M	T	W	T	F	S
1	2	3	4	5	6	7
8	9	10	11	12	13	14
15	16	17	18	19	20	21
22	23	24	25	26	27	28

March 2009

S	M	T	W	T	F	S
1	2	3	4	5	6	7
8	9	10	11	12	13	14
15	16	17	18	19	20	21
22	23	24	25	26	27	28
29	30	31				

April 2009

S	M	T	W	T	F	S
			1	2	3	4
5	6	7	8	9	10	11
12	13	14	15	16	17	18
19	20	21	22	23	24	25
26	27	28	29	30		

May 2009

S	M	T	W	T	F	S
					1	2
3	4	5	6	7	8	9
10	11	12	13	14	15	16
17	18	19	20	21	22	23
24/31	25	26	27	28	29	30

June 2009

S	M	T	W	T	F	S
	1	2	3	4	5	6
7	8	9	10	11	12	13
14	15	16	17	18	19	20
21	22	23	24	25	26	27
28	29	30				

July 2009

S	M	T	W	T	F	S
			1	2	3	4
5	6	7	8	9	10	11
12	13	14	15	16	17	18
19	20	21	22	23	24	25
26	27	28	29	30	31	

August 2009

S	M	T	W	T	F	S
						1
2	3	4	5	6	7	8
9	10	11	12	13	14	15
16	17	18	19	20	21	22
23/30	24/31	25	26	27	28	29

September 2009

S	M	T	W	T	F	S
		1	2	3	4	5
6	7	8	9	10	11	12
13	14	15	16	17	18	19
20	21	22	23	24	25	26
27	28	29	30			

October 2009

S	M	T	W	T	F	S
				1	2	3
4	5	6	7	8	9	10
11	12	13	14	15	16	17
18	19	20	21	22	23	24
25	26	27	28	29	30	31

November 2009

S	M	T	W	T	F	S
1	2	3	4	5	6	7
8	9	10	11	12	13	14
15	16	17	18	19	20	21
22	23	24	25	26	27	28
29	30					

December 2009

S	M	T	W	T	F	S
		1	2	3	4	5
6	7	8	9	10	11	12
13	14	15	16	17	18	19
20	21	22	23	24	25	26
27	28	29	30	31		

Test Prep

Fill in the ○ for the correct answer.

6. Which month comes first?

○ September ○ February ○ August ○ July

Use with text pages 447–448.

Name ______________________ Date ____________

Practice 16.7

Hours, Days, Weeks, and Months

Use the words in the box.
Write the best estimate for the length of the activity.

Think
About how long each activity usually takes.

hours	days	weeks	months

1. A school day

hours

2. Summer vacation

____

3. Growing taller

____

4. A skiing trip

____

5. Seeds to grow

____

____

6. A hiking trip

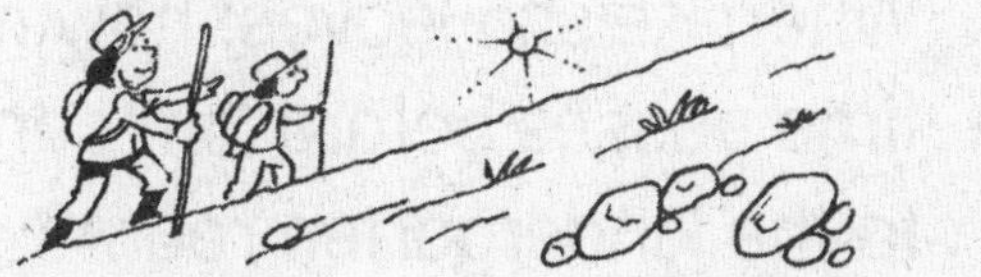

____

Test Prep

7. Write about or draw something that takes weeks to do.

Use with text pages 449–450.

Name ______________________ Date ____________

Practice 16.8

Problem Solving: Use a Table

Some second graders help out in the kindergarten room.

Solve.
Use the table and a clock to help you.

Second Grade Helpers	
Student	**Time**
Keisha	10:00 to 11:00
Molly	10:30 to 11:30
Jim	1:00 to 1:30
Miguel	1:30 to 2:30

	Draw or write to explain.
1. How long does Molly help in the kindergarten? 1 hour or 60 minutes	
2. The kindergarten teacher asks Jim to help until 2:00. How much more time will Jim help? ______	
3. When Keisha leaves, how much time passes before Jim comes to the kindergarten room? ______	

Test Prep

4. Look at the table. Who spends less time on homework?

Claire	Kim
3:00 to 3:30	3:00 to 5:00

______

Use with text pages 451–453.

Name ____________________ Date __________

Practice 17.1

Nonstandard Units

Find the real object.

Use paper clip and square unit.

Estimate the length with each unit.

Then measure.

Object	Estimate	Measure
1. 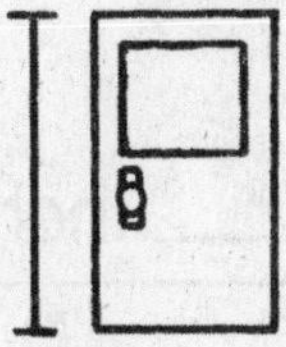	about ____ about ____	about ____ about ____
2. 	about ____ about ____	about ____ about ____
3. 	about ____ about ____	about ____ about ____
4. 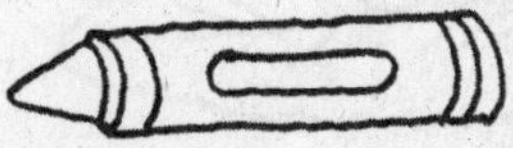	about ____ about ____	about ____ about ____

Test Prep

Fill in the ○ for the correct answer. NH means Not Here.

5. About how many paper clips long is this pencil?

1	3	10	NH
○	○	○	○

Use with text pages 475–478.

Name ______________________ Date ____________

Practice 17.2

Activity: Inches

Find the real object. Estimate the length.
Then use a ruler to measure to the nearest inch.

	Object	Estimate	Measure
1.		about ______ inches	about ______ inches
2.		about ______ inches	about ______ inches
3.		about ______ inches	about ______ inches

Find an object to measure in inches.
Estimate its length. Then use a ruler to measure it to the nearest inch.

4. ______________ about ______ inches about ______ inches

Compare. Circle the longer object.

5.

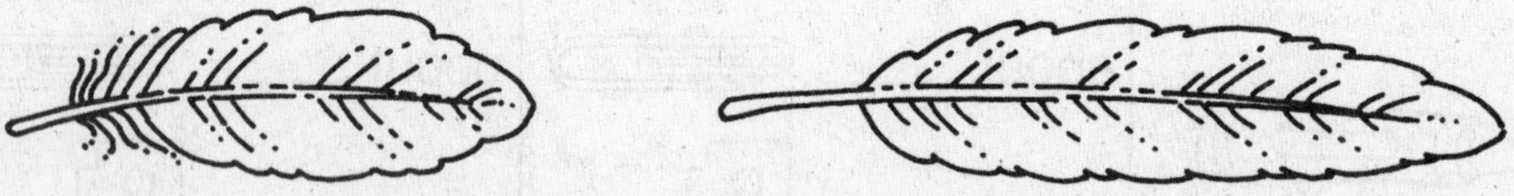

Test Prep

6. Measure the marker.

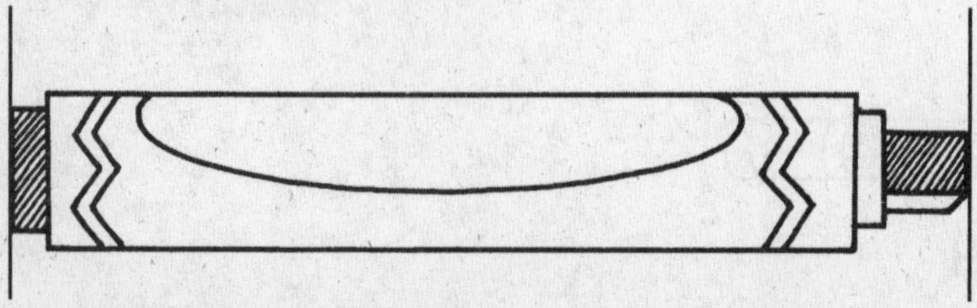

The marker is about _____ inches.

Use with text pages 479–481.

Name ______________________ Date ____________

Practice 17.3

Activity: Inches and Feet

Find the real object. Use inches or feet.
Estimate. Then measure.

	Object	Estimate	Measure
1.	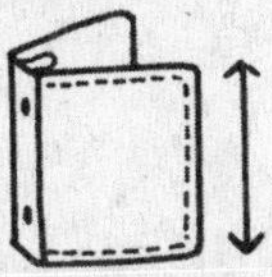	about ______ ______	about ______ ______
2.		about ______ ______	about ______ ______

Draw an object to measure.
Use inches or feet. Estimate. Then measure.

	Draw the object	Estimate	Measure
3.		about ______ ______	about ______ ______
4.		about ______ ______	about ______ ______

Test Prep

Circle the answer.

5. Which is the better estimate for the real object?

2 inches

2 feet

Use with text pages 483–484.

Name ____________________ Date __________

Foot and Yard

Use feet or yards to estimate.
Then measure.

Find	Estimate	Measure
1. How far apart? 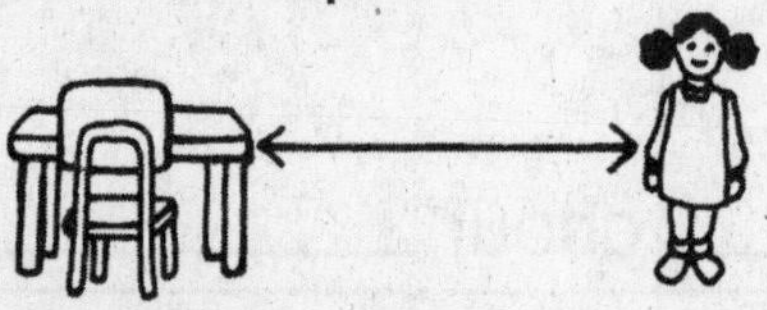	about _____ yards	about _____ yards
2. How wide? 	about _____ _____	about _____ _____
3. How tall? 	about _____ _____	about _____ _____
4. How tall? 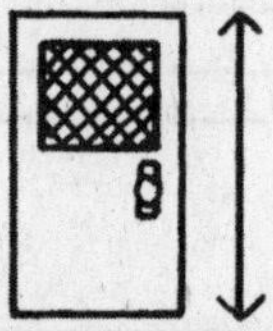	about _____ _____	about _____ _____
5. How wide? 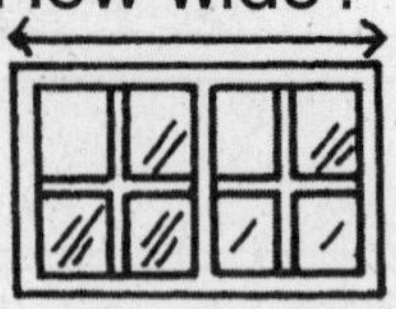	about _____ _____	about _____ _____

Test Prep

Circle the answer.

6. Which is the better estimate for the real object?

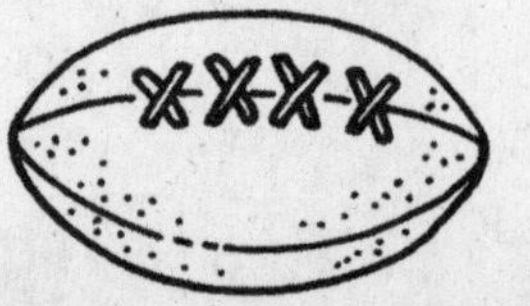

1 foot

1 yard

Use with text pages 485–486.

Name ______________________ Date ______________

Practice 17.5

Centimeters and Meters

Find the real object.
Use centimeters or meters.
Estimate. Then measure.

Remember
Label your answers with cm or m.

Object	Estimate	Measure
1. 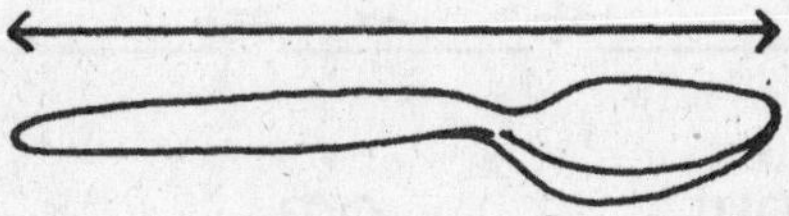	about ______ ______	about ______ ______
2. 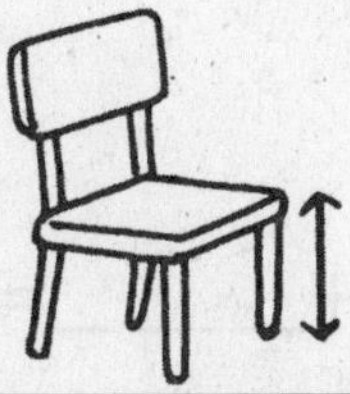	about ______ ______	about ______ ______
3. 	about ______ ______	about ______ ______
4. 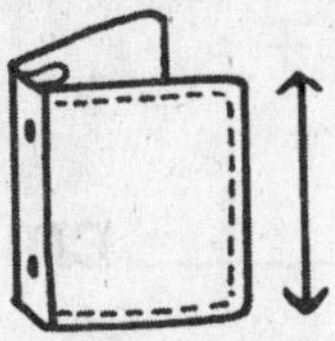	about ______ ______	about ______ ______

5. Look at the lengths of the four objects you measured.
Write the lengths from longest to shortest.

____________ ____________ ____________ ____________

Test Prep

Fill in the ○ for the correct answer.

6. Which is something that would be measured in meters?

shoe ○ bulletin board ○ worm ○ hand ○

Use with text pages 489–490.

Name ______________________ Date ____________

Perimeter

Find the real object. Use a centimeter ruler.
Measure and write the length of each side.
Add to find the perimeter.

Remember
Measure to the nearest centimeter.

1. 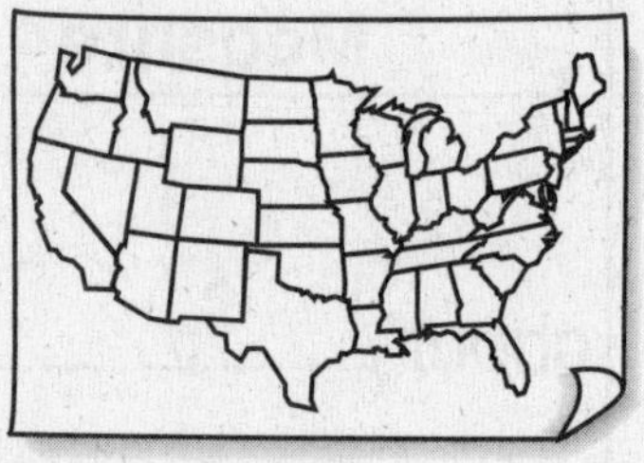

_____ + _____ + _____ + _____ = _____ cm

The perimeter is about _____ cm.

2. 

_____ + _____ + _____ + _____ = _____ cm

The perimeter is about _____ cm.

3. 

_____ + _____ + _____ + _____ = _____ cm

The perimeter is about _____ cm.

4. 

_____ + _____ + _____ + _____ = _____ cm

The perimeter is about _____ cm.

Test Prep

Fill in the ○ for the correct answer.

5. Which is the perimeter of the rectangle?

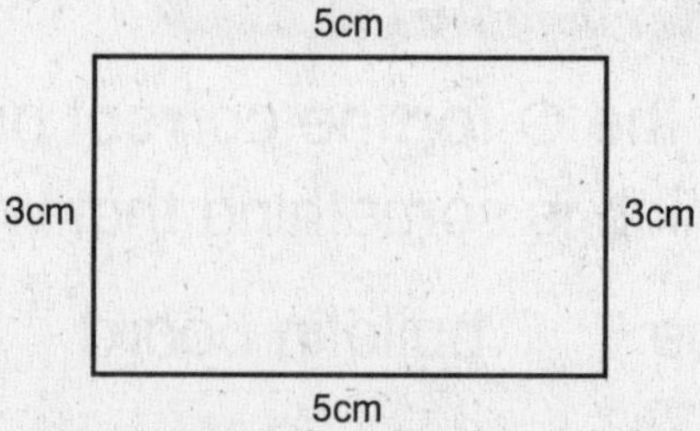

16 cm	10 cm	6 cm	4 cm
○	○	○	○

Use with text pages 491–492.

Name ______________________ Date ____________

Practice 17.7

Activity: Area

Use square units.
Estimate. Then find the area of the shape.

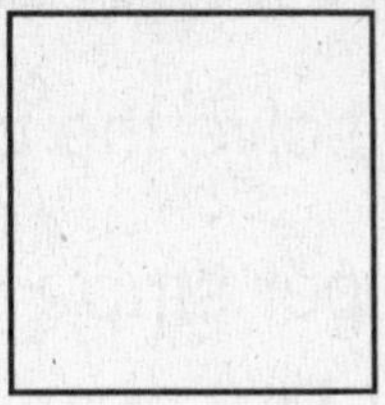

1.

Estimate: about ______ square units

Measure: about __9__ square units

2.

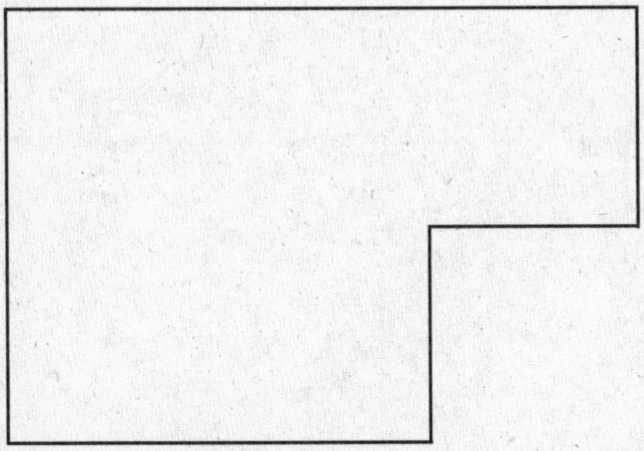

Estimate: about ______ square units

Measure: about ______ square units

Test Prep

3. Kristen made a book cover. It is 9 square units long and 5 square units wide. What is the area of her book cover?

______________ square units

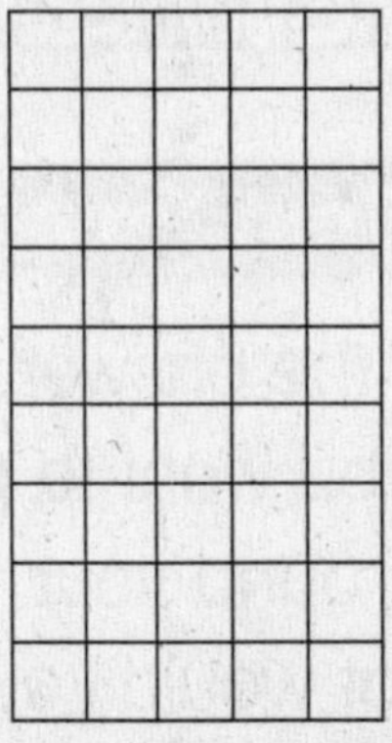

Use with text pages 493–495.

Name ______________________ Date ____________

Practice 17.8

Problem Solving: Use a Picture

Use the picture to solve the problem. Draw or write to explain.

1. Joan made a paper strip frame for her picture.
How much paper did Joan use?

40 cm

2. Barry wants to make a bookmark just like this one.
How long will it be? Measure.

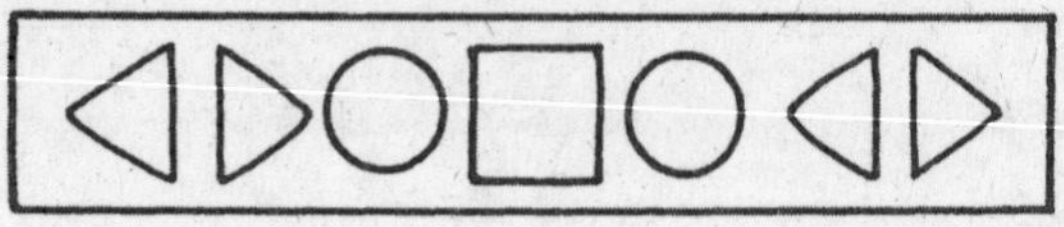

______ cm

3. Lisa wants to make this quilt.
How many square patches will she need?

______ square patches

Test Prep

Circle the answer.

4. If you want to put up a fence to surround your front yard, what would you need to find?

perimeter area

Name ______________________ Date ____________

Practice 18.1

Activity: Cups, Pints, Quarts, and Gallons

Remember
2 cups = 1 pint
2 pints = 1 quart
4 quarts = 1 gallon

Use cup, pint, quart, and gallon containers.
Find out which amount is greater. Circle it.
Circle both if they are the same.

1. 5 quarts 1 gallon
2. 6 pints 12 cups
3. 5 pints 2 quarts
4. 1 quart 3 cups
5. 16 cups 1 gallon
6. 2 gallons 7 quarts

Find the container and the measuring tool.
Estimate. Then measure to the nearest unit.

	Container	Estimate	Measure
7.	plastic jug	about _____ quarts	about _____ quarts
8.	small bowl	about _____ cups	about _____ cups
9.	cooking pot	about _____ gallons	about _____ gallons

Test Prep

Fill in the ○ for the correct answer.

10. Which number makes the sentence true?

6 cups = _____ pints

2	3	4	6
○	○	○	○

Use with text pages 507–509.

Name ______________________ Date ____________

Practice 18.2

Activity: Liters

Find the container.
Estimate how many liters it holds.
Measure.

	Container	Estimate	Measure
1.	bucket	about ____ liters	about ____ liters
2.	vase	about ____ liters	about ____ liters
3.	waste basket	about ____ liters	about ____ liters

Remember
A milliliter is a very small amount.

Circle the better estimate.

4. 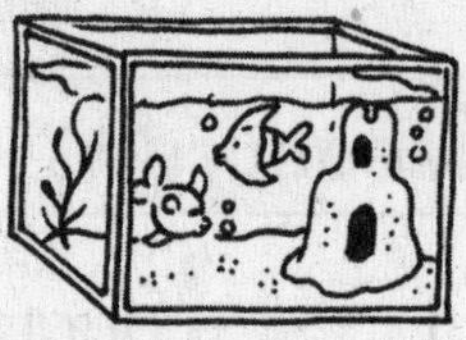

10 liters   10 milliliters

5. 

50 liters   50 milliliters

Test Prep

Fill in the ○ for the correct answer. NH means Not Here.

6. This cooking pot holds about how much water?

I liter	10 milliliters	3 liters	NH
○	○	○	○

Use with text pages 511–512.

Name ______________________ Date ____________

Practice 18.3

Activity: Pounds and Ounces

You can measure weight in pounds and ounces.

about 1 pound

more than 1 pound

Find objects that weigh more than 1 pound.
Write their names in the table.
Estimate the weight to the nearest pound.
Use a balance scale and a 1-pound measure to check.

Object Name	Estimate	Measure
1. ____________	about ____ pounds	about ____ pounds
2. ____________	about ____ pounds	about ____ pounds
3. ____________	about ____ pounds	about ____ pounds
4. ____________	about ____ pounds	about ____ pounds

5. Write the four weights in order from lightest to heaviest.

____ pounds ____ pounds ____ pounds ____ pounds

Test Prep

6. Circle the answer. Which is the best estimate?

A dog weighs ____________.

less than 1 pound about 10 ounces more than 1 pound

Use with text pages 513–514.

Name ______________________ Date ______________

Activity: Kilograms and Grams

Use a balance scale and objects that are 1 kilogram and 1 gram.
Complete the table.
Write **more than**, **less than**, or **about**.

Object	Estimate	Measure
1. math book	________ 1 kilogram	more than 1 kilogram
2. sheet of paper	________ 1 gram	________ 1 gram
3. dictionary	________ 1 gram	________ 1 gram

Find objects that are more than 1 kilogram.
Write their names in the table.
Estimate. Then measure.

Object Name	Estimate	Measure
4. ____________	about _____ kilograms	about _____ kilograms
5. ____________	about _____ kilograms	about _____ kilograms
6. ____________	about _____ kilograms	about _____ kilograms

Test Prep

7. Circle the picture.
Which is more than 1 kilogram?

Use with text pages 515–516.

Name ______________________ Date ____________

Temperature: Fahrenheit

Write the temperature.

Remember
From one line to the next is 2 degrees.

1.

24 °F

2.

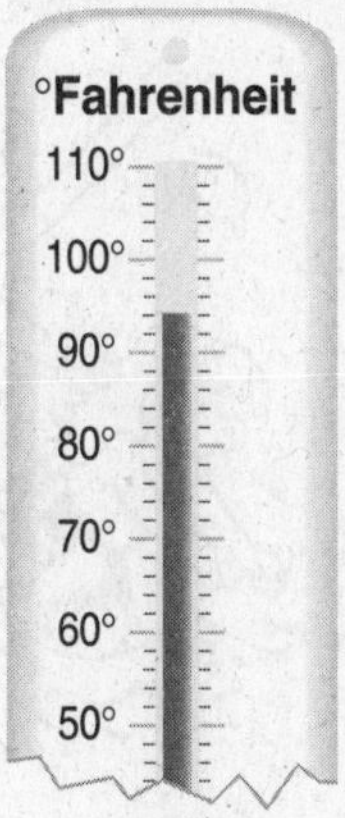

_____ °F

3.

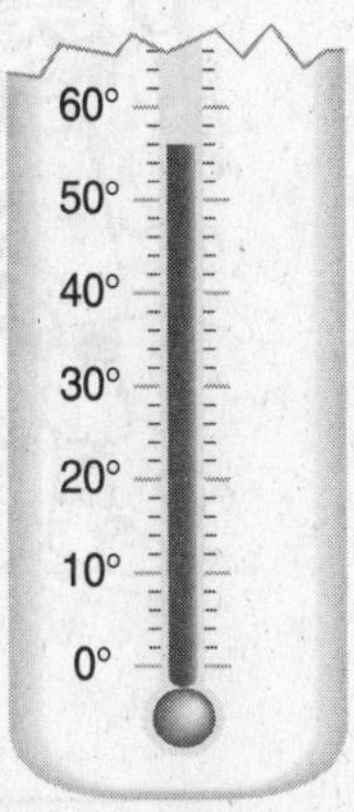

_____ °F

4.

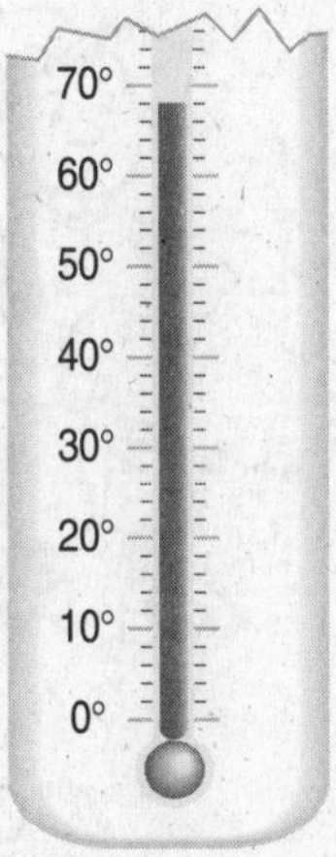

_____ °F

Test Prep

Fill in the ○ for the correct answer. NH means Not Here.

5. What is the temperature?

Rico chooses a coat and mittens to wear to school.

37°F	60°F	75°F	NH
○	○	○	○

Use with text pages 519–520.

Name ______________________ Date ____________

Practice 18.6

Temperature: Celsius

Remember
From one line to the next, the temperature changes 5 degrees.

Write the temperature.

1.

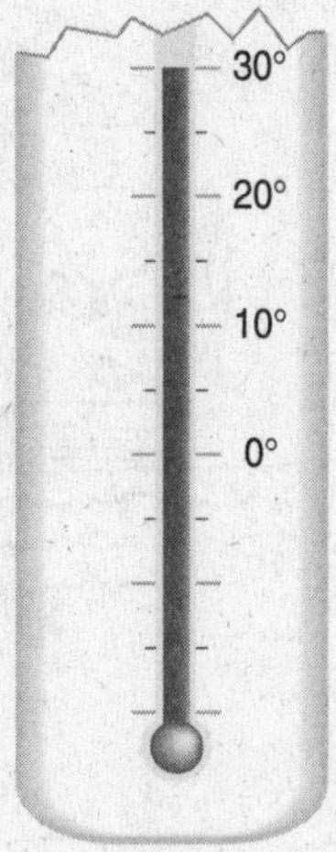

30 °C

2.

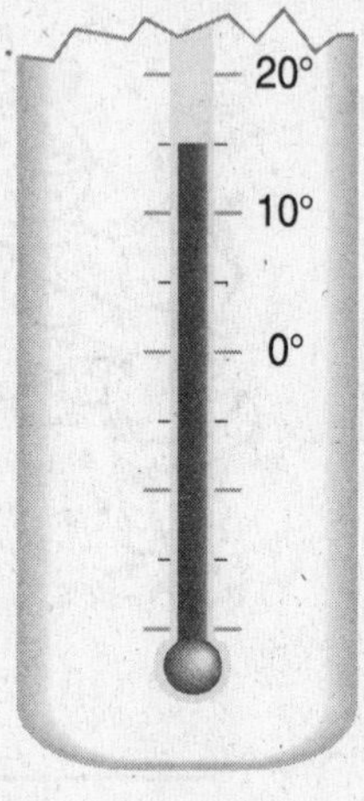

_____ °C

3.

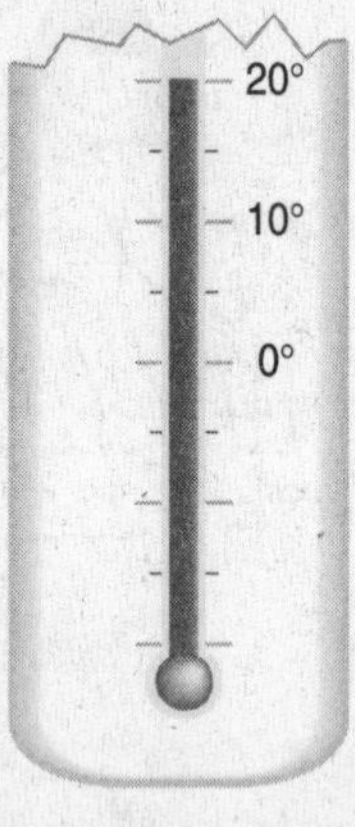

_____ °C

4.

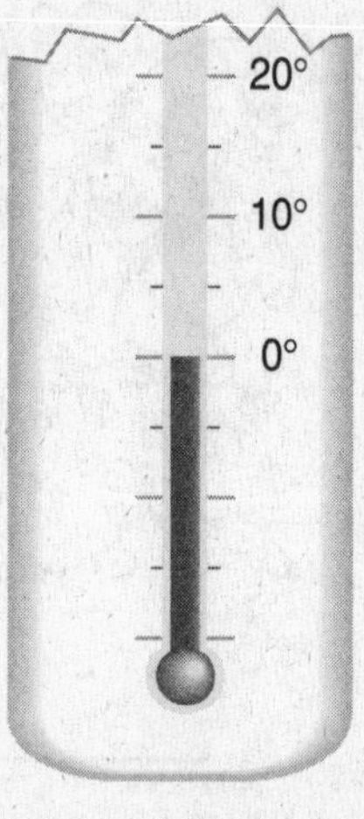

_____ °C

Test Prep

Fill in the ○ for the correct answer.

5. Tasha reads a Celsius thermometer. It is a very cold winter day.
Which temperature does she read?

30°C	25°C	10°C	0°C
○	○	○	○

Use with text pages 521–522.

Name ______________________ Date ____________

Practice 18.7

Measuring Units and Tools

Circle the unit needed to measure.
Then circle the correct tool.

Think
What am I going to measure?

1. How heavy is the fruit?		liter °F centimeter pound	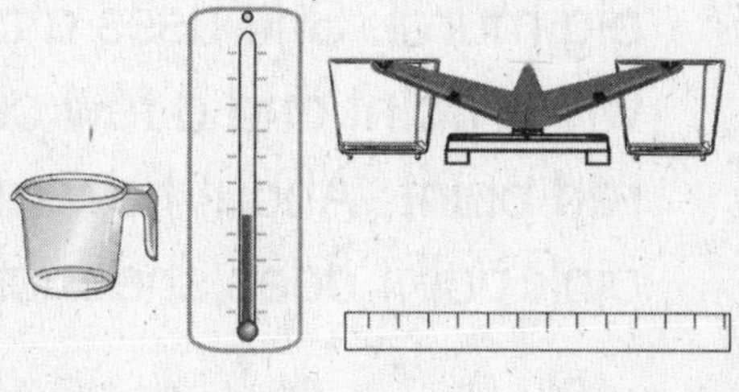
2. How much does the glass hold?	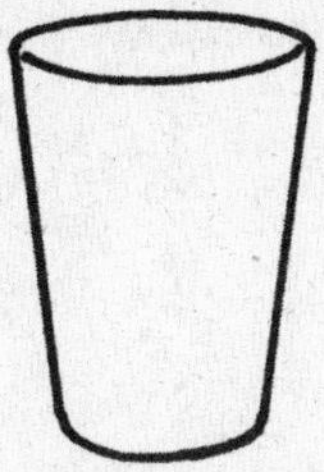	cup °C inch kilogram	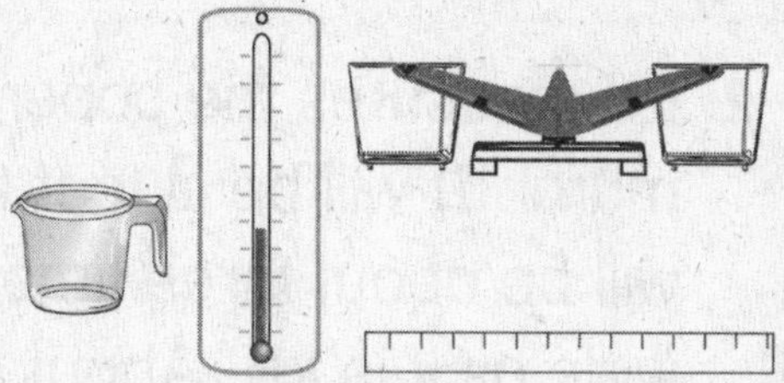
3. How tall is the plant?		liter °F centimeter pound	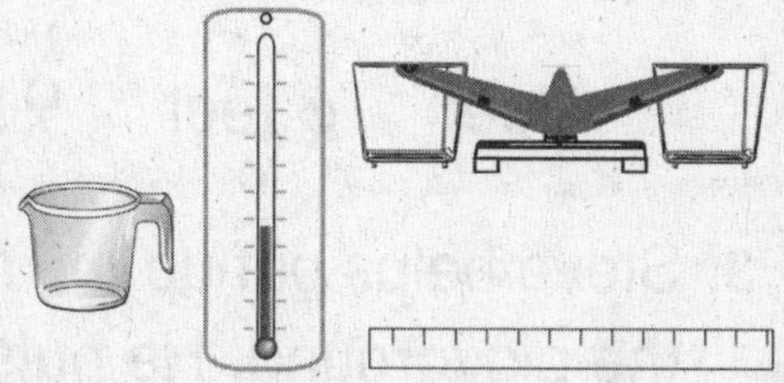
4. What is the temperature today?		gallon °C inch kilogram	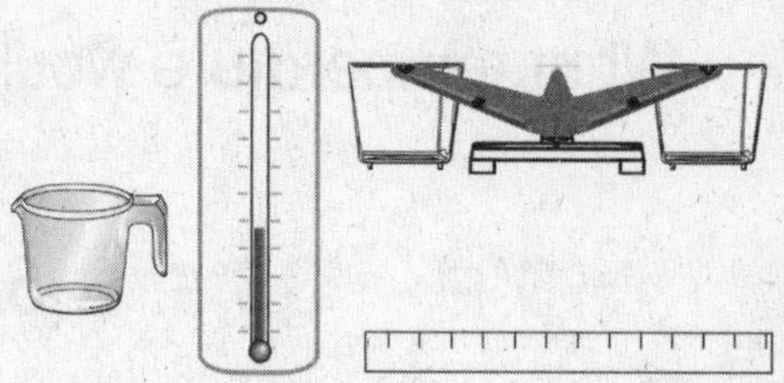

Test Prep

Fill in the ○ for the correct answer.

5. What does the tool measure?

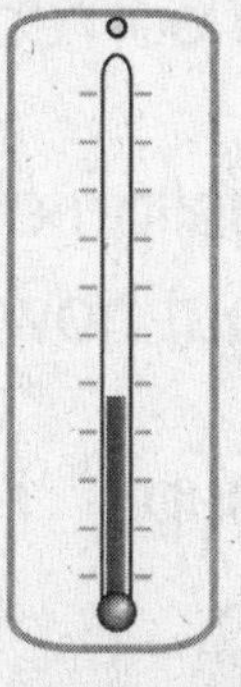

inch	pound	°C	liter
○	○	○	○

Use with text pages 523–524.

Name ____________________ Date __________

Practice 18.8

Problem Solving: Reasonable Answers

Circle the most reasonable answer.

Draw or write to explain.

1. Sophie makes pink paint for a big mural. She uses a cup of white paint and a few cups of red paint. About how much pink paint does she make?

   2 cups   2 pints   2 quarts

2. Ed measures the paper for the mural. It will be 3 feet tall. It will be about three times as wide as it is tall. About how wide will the mural be?

   4 feet   6 feet   9 feet

3. Steve helps put up the mural in the playground. He puts it up on a sunny day in the fall. What temperature would it be?

   10°F   35°F   50°F

Test Prep

Fill in the ○ for the correct answer. NH means Not Here.

4. Simon has a gallon of juice. He pours several cups of juice out for the class. About how much juice does he have left?

   1 milliliter ○   1 cup ○   1 gallon ○   NH ○

Use with text pages 525–526.

Name ____________________ Date ____________

Practice 19.1

Activity: Exploring Multiplication

Use a number line or add equal groups.
Write the answer.

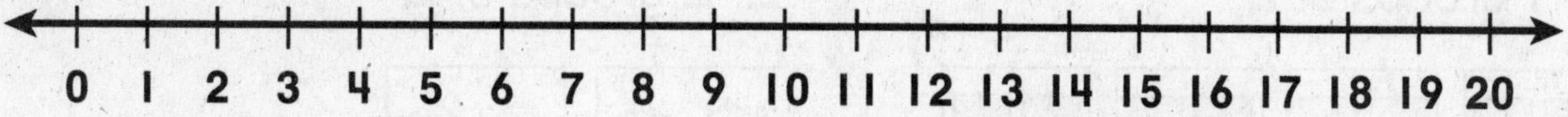

1. 3 groups of 2

6

2. 2 groups of 5

______

3. 10 groups of 2

______

4. 2 groups of 6

______

5. 2 groups of 4

______

6. 4 groups of 5

______

Test Prep

Fill in the ○ for the correct answer.
NH means Not Here.

7. Which number sentence does the number line show?

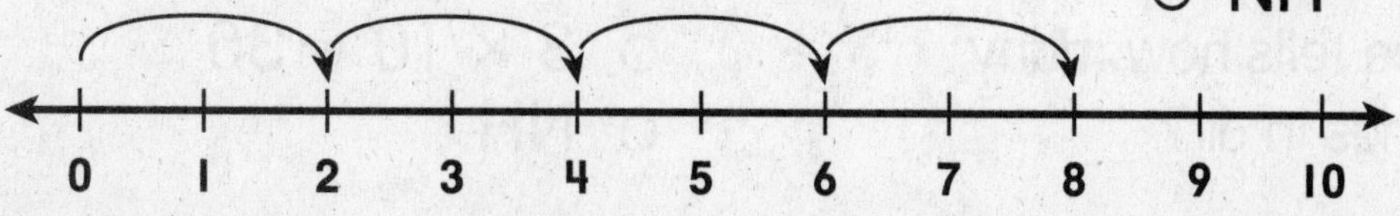

○ 2 + 6 = 8

○ 2 + 2 + 2 + 2 = 8

○ 2 + 4 + 6 + 8 = 20

○ NH

Use with text pages 547–548.

Name ______________________ Date ____________

Practice 19.2

Repeated Addition and Multiplication

Find the sum. Then find the product.

1. 4 groups of 2

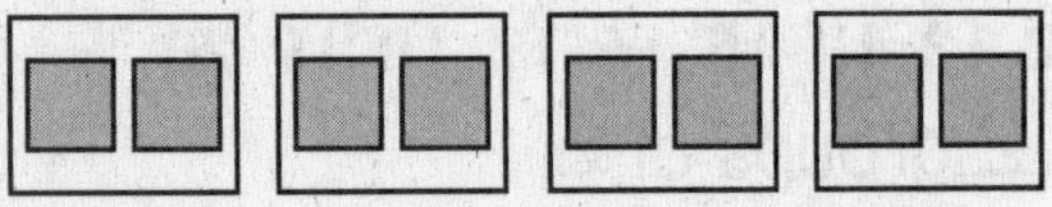

$2 + 2 + 2 + 2 =$ 8

$4 \times 2 =$ 8

2. 2 groups of 2

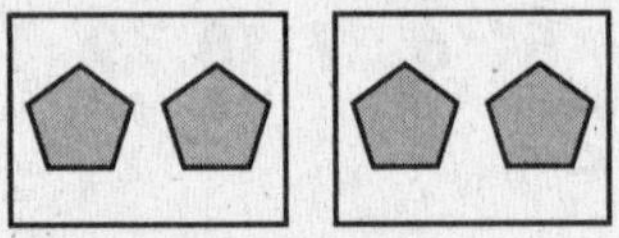

$2 + 2 =$ ____

$2 \times 2 =$ ____

3. 3 groups of 5

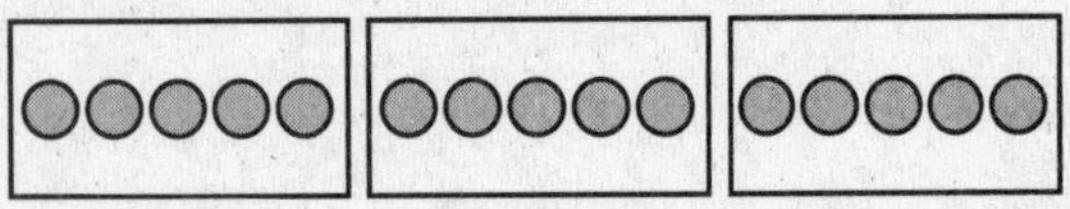

$5 + 5 + 5 =$ ____

$3 \times 5 =$ ____

4. 4 groups of 5

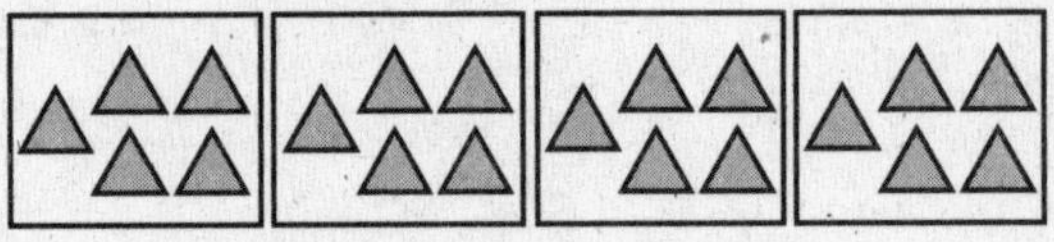

$5 + 5 + 5 + 5 =$ ____

$4 \times 5 =$ ____

Multiply.

5. $4 \times 3 =$ ____ **6.** $1 \times 2 =$ ____ **7.** $4 \times 4 =$ ____

Test Prep

Fill in the ○ for the correct answer.
NH means Not Here.

8. Kayla has 3 boxes of muffins. There are 10 muffins in each box. Which sentence tells how many muffins Kayla has in all?

- ○ $3 + 10 = 13$
- ○ $3 \times 5 = 15$
- ○ $3 \times 10 = 30$
- ○ NH

Use with text pages 549–550.

Name ______________________ Date ____________

Practice 19.3

Skip Count to Multiply

Draw ants. Skip-count. Then find the product.

1. 2 groups of 4 ants

$2 \times 4 =$ 8 ants in all

2. 3 groups of 5 ants

$3 \times 5 =$ ______ ants in all

3. 3 groups of 3 ants

$3 \times 3 =$ ______ ants in all

4. 4 groups of 2 ants

$4 \times 2 =$ ______ ants in all

5. 2 groups of 10 ants

$2 \times 10 =$ ______ ants in all

6. 4 groups of 4 ants

$4 \times 4 =$ ______ ants in all

Multiply.

7. $3 \times 10 =$ ______
8. $6 \times 2 =$ ______
9. $7 \times 5 =$ ______

Test Prep

Fill in the ○ for the correct answer.

10. Which multiplication sentence tells about this picture?

$3 \times 10 = 30$	$3 \times 5 = 15$	$2 \times 10 = 20$	$2 \times 4 = 8$
○	○	○	○

Use with text pages 551–552.

Name ______________________ Date ______________

Practice 19.4

Multiply with Arrays

Use Learning Tool 46 and counters.

Draw the counters to make equal rows. Find the product.

1. 3 rows of 2   2 rows of 3

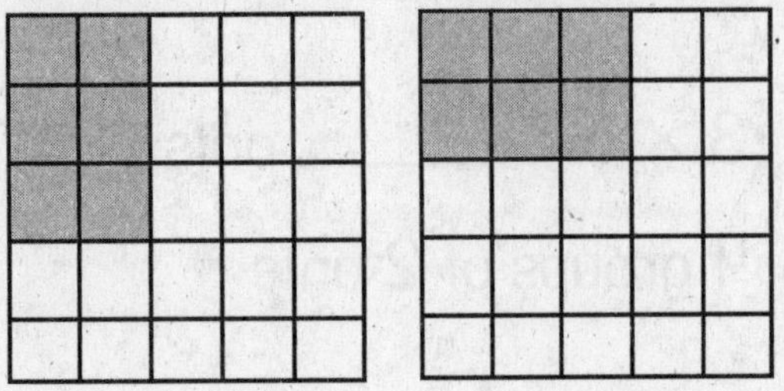

3 × 2 = 6   2 × 3 = 6

2. 3 rows of 5   5 rows of 3

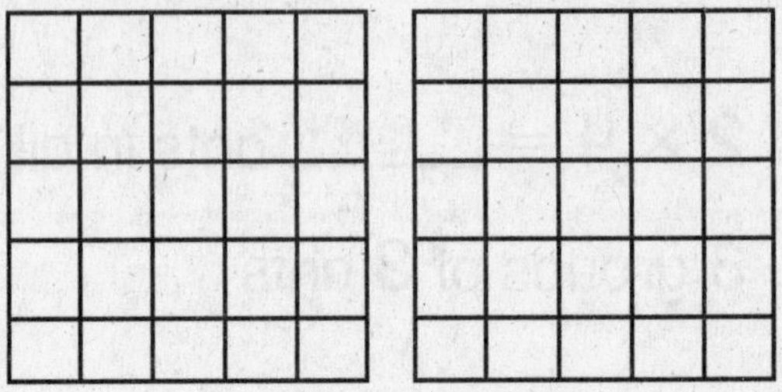

3 × 5 = _____   5 × 3 = _____

Use Learning Tool 46 and counters. Complete the number sentence.

3. **3** rows of **4**   **4** rows of **3**

_____ × _____ = _____ or _____ × _____ = _____

Multiply.

4.

4 × 5 = _____   5 × 4 = _____

5.

1 × 2 = _____   2 × 1 = _____

6.

6 × 5 = _____   5 × 6 = _____

7.

10 × 3 = _____   3 × 10 = _____

Test Prep

Fill in the ○ for the correct answer. NH means Not Here.

8. Which number will make the number sentence true?

2 × 4 = □ × 2

2	4	8	NH
○	○	○	○

Use with text pages 553–555.

Name ______________________ Date ____________

Practice 19.5

Make and Use a Multiplication Table

×	0	1	2	3	4	5
0	0	0	0	0	0	0
1	0	1	2	3	4	5
2	0	2	4	6	8	10
3	0	3	6	9	12	15
4	0	4	8	12	16	20
5	0	5	10	15	20	25

Use the multiplication table. Find each product.

1. $3 \times 2 =$ 6
2. $1 \times 4 =$ ______
3. $5 \times 3 =$ ______
4. $0 \times 4 =$ ______
5. $5 \times 5 =$ ______
6. $3 \times 3 =$ ______
7. $2 \times 1 =$ ______
8. $4 \times 3 =$ ______
9. $2 \times 4 =$ ______

Look for patterns in the table.

10. Color the row and column that count by 2 blue.
11. Color the row and column that count by 3 yellow.

Test Prep

12. Two numbers have a product of 10 and a sum of 7. What are the numbers?

Draw or write to explain.

______

______ × ______ = ______

______ + ______ = ______

Use with text pages 557–558.

Name ____________________ Date ____________

Activity: Share Equally

Use Workmat 1 and counters.
Draw dots to show the number in each group.
Write how many are in each group.

1. 6 counters
   3 groups

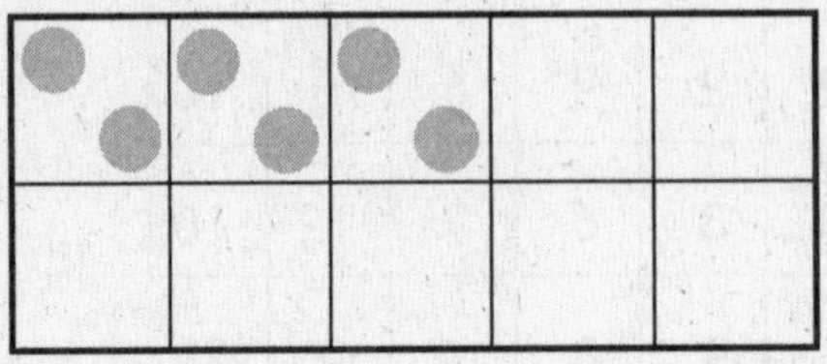

$6 \div 3 =$ 2

2 in each group

2. 8 counters
   2 groups

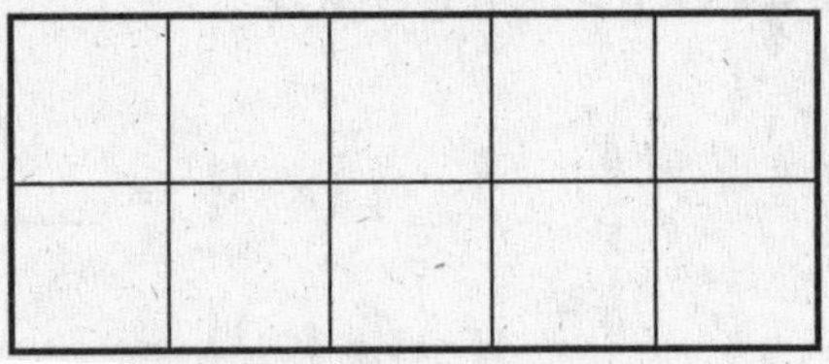

$8 \div 2 =$ ____

____ in each group

3. 15 counters
   5 groups

$15 \div 5 =$ ____

____ in each group

Test Prep

Fill in the ○ for the correct answer.
NH means Not Here.

4. There are 15 pencils to put in 3 boxes. Bob puts the same number in each box. Which number sentence tells how many pencils are in each box?

   ○ $15 \div 5 = 3$
   ○ $15 \div 3 = 5$
   ○ $15 - 3 = 12$
   ○ NH

Use with text pages 561–562.

Name ______________________ Date ____________

Practice 19.7

Make Equal Groups

Circle groups of 2.
Complete the division sentence.

1.

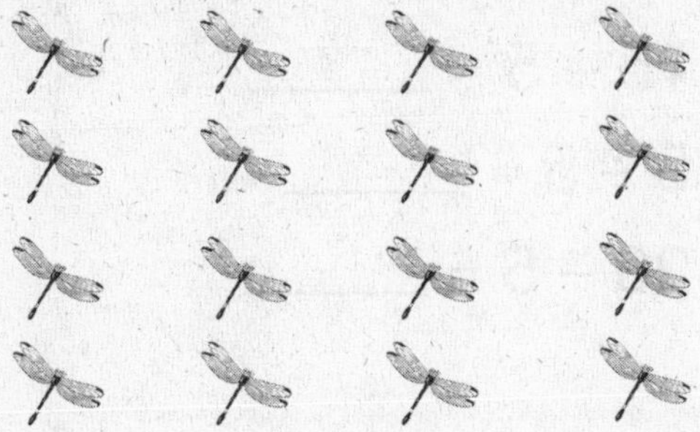

16 ÷ 2 = 8

2.

____ ÷ ____ = ____

Circle groups of 5.
Complete the division sentence.

3.

____ ÷ ____ = ____

4.

____ ÷ ____ = ____

Test Prep

Solve.

5. Annie has 25 flowers to put in baskets. She wants to make equal groups of 5 flowers. How many groups will she make?

Draw or write to explain.

____ groups

Use with text pages 563–564.

Name ______________________ Date ______________

Practice 19.8

Use Repeated Subtraction

Subtract by 5s to divide by 5.
Use the number line on Workmat 4 to divide.

1. 25 ÷ 5 = 5
2. 15 ÷ 5 = ______
3. 45 ÷ 5 = ______
4. 5 ÷ 5 = ______
5. 30 ÷ 5 = ______
6. 20 ÷ 5 = ______

Subtract by 2s to divide by 2.
Use the number line on Workmat 4 to divide.

7. 8 ÷ 2 = ______
8. 12 ÷ 2 = ______
9. 4 ÷ 2 = ______
10. 14 ÷ 2 = ______
11. 16 ÷ 2 = ______
12. 6 ÷ 2 = ______

Test Prep

Fill in the ○ for the correct answer.
NH means Not Here.

13. Which division fact can be solved by subtracting 5 from 10 two times?

5 ÷ 2	10 ÷ 5	10 ÷ 1	NH
○	○	○	○

Use with text pages 565–566.

Name ______________________ Date ____________

Practice 19.9

Problem Solving: Draw a Picture

Draw a picture to solve.

Draw or write to explain.

1. There are 5 shirts in Joe's closet. Each shirt has 5 buttons. How many buttons are there in all?

25 buttons

2. There are 3 bags. Each bag has 4 apples. How many apples are there in all?

_____ apples

3. Mrs. Super's class has 30 children. The class is divided into 5 equal groups. How many children are in each group?

_____ children

Test Prep

Fill in the ○ for the correct answer.

4. Mr. Han makes 18 wooden toys. He puts an equal number of toys in 2 boxes. How many toys does he put in each box?

2 toys	9 toys	16 toys	20 toys
○	○	○	○

Use with text pages 567–569.

Name ______________________ Date ____________

Practice 20.1

Hundreds and Tens

Count by hundreds and tens.
Write the number.

1. 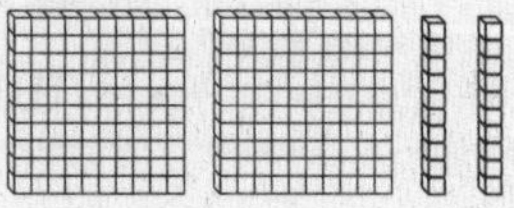

2 hundreds 2 tens

220 two hundred twenty

2. 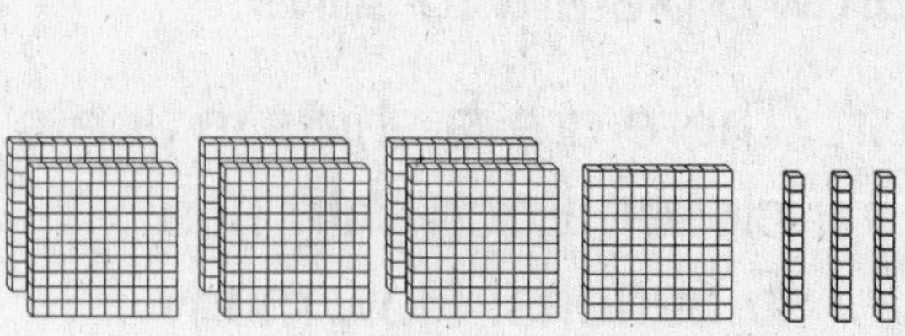

_____ hundreds _____ tens

________ seven hundred thirty

3. 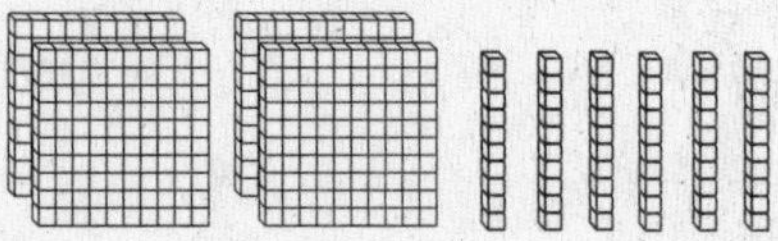

_____ hundreds _____ tens

________ four hundred sixty

4. 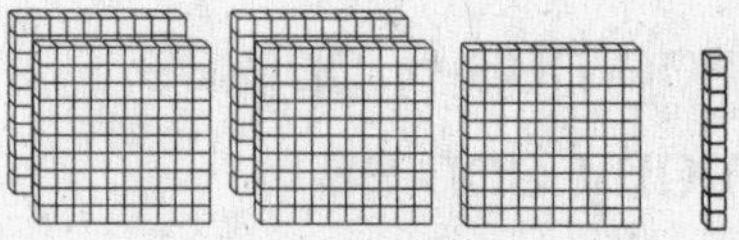

_____ hundreds _____ tens

________ five hundred ten

5. 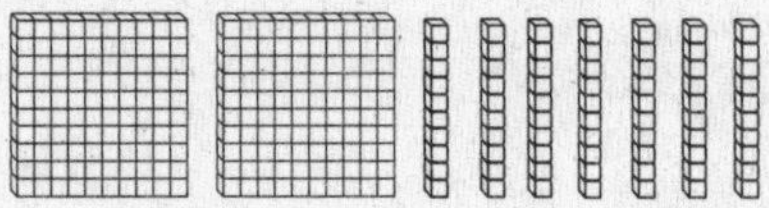

_____ hundreds _____ tens

________ two hundred seventy

6. 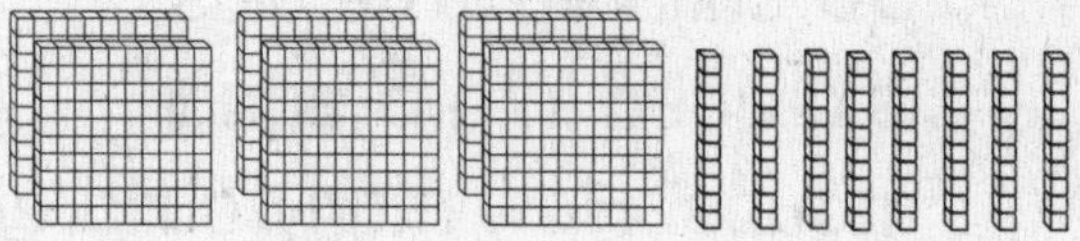

_____ hundreds _____ tens

________ six hundred eighty

Test Prep

Fill in the ○ for the correct answer.
NH means Not Here.

7. Which number is 100 more than 759?

659	769	859	NH
○	○	○	○

Use with text pages 577–579.

Name ______________________ Date ____________

Hundreds, Tens, and Ones

Use Workmat 6 with 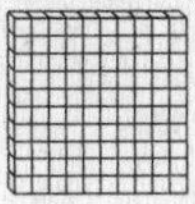, , and .

Show this many.	Write how many.	Write the number.
1. 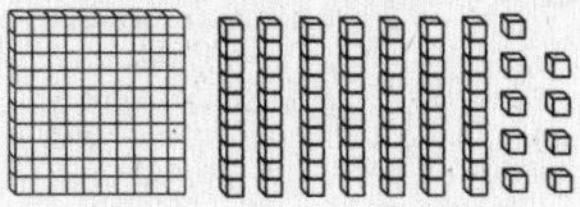	Hundreds: 1 / Tens: 7 / Ones: 9	179 one hundred seventy nine
2. 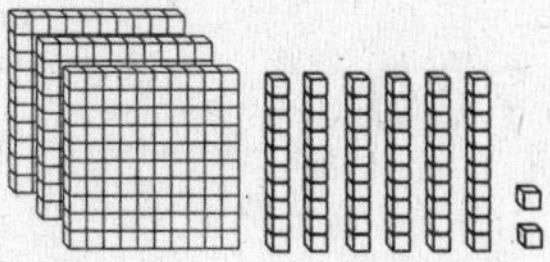	Hundreds: ___ / Tens: ___ / Ones: ___	______ three hundred sixty-two
3. 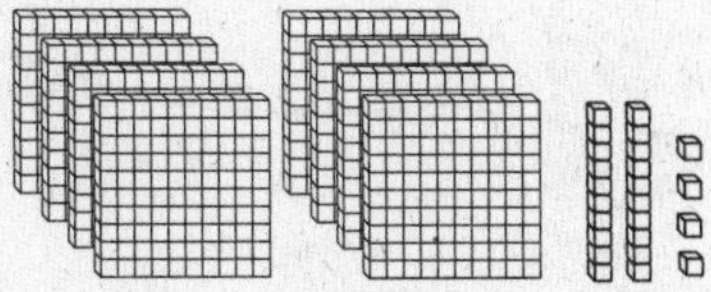	Hundreds: ___ / Tens: ___ / Ones: ___	______ eight hundred twenty-four
4. 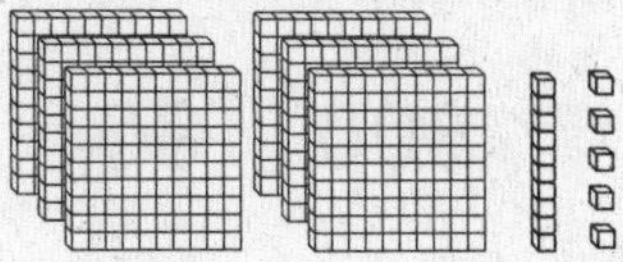	Hundreds: ___ / Tens: ___ / Ones: ___	______ six hundred fifteen

Test Prep

Fill in the ○ for the correct answer.
NH means Not Here.

5. Which number does the model show?

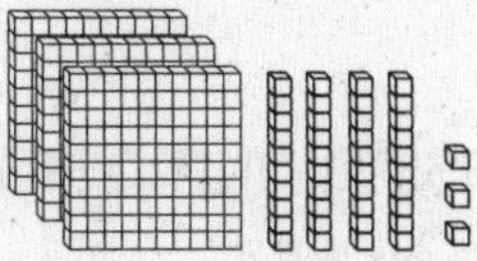

○ 300
○ 334
○ 343
○ NH

Use with text pages 581–582.

Name ______________________ Date ____________

Practice 20.3

Identify Place Value to 1,000

Write the number.

1. 7 + 40 + 300 347	2. 400 + 8 ______
3. 9 + 50 + 400 ______	4. 600 + 20 + 1 ______
5. 20 + 100 ______	6. 1 + 30 + 200 ______
7. 900 + 9 ______	8. 4 + 50 + 700 ______

Circle the value of the underlined digit.

To find the value of a digit, find the value of its place.

9. 6̲31	600	60	6	10. 12̲7	200	20	2
11. 503̲	300	30	3	12. 8̲45	800	80	8
13. 29̲0	900	90	9	14. 762̲	200	20	2

Test Prep

Fill in the ○ for the correct answer.
NH means Not Here.

15. Count by 50. What are the missing numbers?

200, 250, 300, 350, ____, 450, ____

○ 350, 450

○ 400, 500

○ 450, 550

○ NH

Use with text pages 583–584.

Name ______________________ Date ____________

Practice 20.4

Read and Write Numbers Through 1,000

Write the number.

1. eighteen 18
2. nine hundred fifty-four ____
3. seven hundred seventy-six ____
4. eighty-two ____
5. nine hundred two ____
6. two hundred forty-two ____
7. thirteen ____
8. eighty-seven ____
9. one hundred sixty-six ____
10. three hundred twenty-nine ____

Circle the word name for the number.

11.	62	sixty-two	ninety-two
12.	684	six hundred eighty-four	eight hundred forty-six
13.	507	fifty-seven	five hundred seven
14.	199	nine hundred ninety-nine	one hundred ninety-nine
15.	567	five hundred sixty-seven	five hundred seventy-six
16.	747	seven hundred forty	seven hundred forty-seven

Test Prep

Fill in the ○ for the correct answer.
NH means Not Here.

17. What is the value of the underlined digit?

2<u>3</u>0

○ two hundred
○ thirty
○ twenty-three
○ NH

Use with text pages 585–586.

Name ______________________ Date ____________

Practice 20.5

Different Ways to Show Numbers

Circle another way to show the number.

1. 324	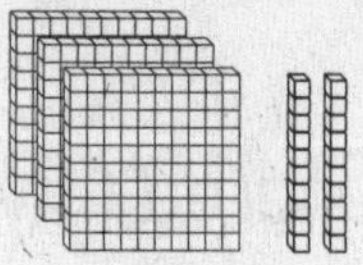	300 + 20 + 4
2. 490	4 hundreds 9 tens	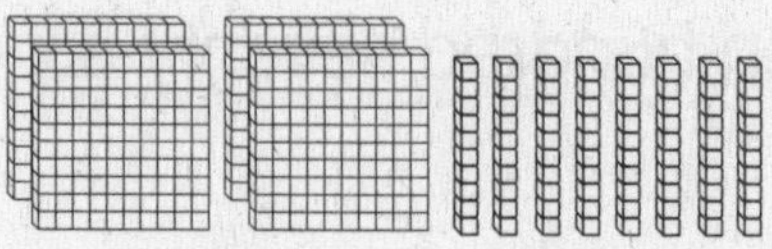
3. 113	100 + 30 + 1	1 hundred 1 ten 3 ones
4. 936	900 + 30 + 6	9 hundreds 6 tens 3 ones

Draw or write to show the number another way.

5. 362

6. 203

Test Prep

Solve.

7. Paul has 3 boxes with 100 pencils in each box. He has 4 boxes with 10 pencils in each. He has 1 box with 5 pencils. How many pencils does he have?

Draw or write to explain.

_______ pencils

Use with text pages 587–588.

Name ______________________ Date ____________

Before, After, Between

Write the number.

	Before	Between	After
1.	380, 381	393, 394, 395	386, 387
2.	____, 386	391, ____, 393	389, ____
3.	____, 390	389, ____, 391	391, ____
4.	____, 388	385, ____, 387	380, ____

Write the missing numbers.

5. 101, ____, ____, 104, 105, 106, ____, ____

6. 890, ____, 892, 893, 894, 895, ____, ____

7. 25, 26, ____, 28, ____, ____, 31, 32, ____

8. 364, 365, 366, ____, ____, 369, ____, 371

Test Prep

Fill in the ○ for the correct answer.

9. Harry is thinking of 2 numbers. They are between 184 and 187. What are the numbers?

- ○ 183 and 184
- ○ 184 and 185
- ○ 185 and 186
- ○ 186 and 187

Use with text pages 591–592.

Name ____________________ Date __________

Compare and Order 3-Digit Numbers

Compare the numbers.
Write >, <, or = in the ◯.

1. 741 (>) 544	2. 913 ◯ 903	3. 460 ◯ 355
4. 799 ◯ 800	5. 429 ◯ 249	6. 850 ◯ 895
7. 864 ◯ 846	8. 667 ◯ 695	9. 311 ◯ 113

Write the numbers in order from least to greatest.

10. 648 700 685 658 ______ ______ ______ ______

11. 900 967 876 970 ______ ______ ______ ______

Write the numbers in order from greatest to least.

12. 267 284 270 262 ______ ______ ______ ______

13. 714 670 706 760 ______ ______ ______ ______

Test Prep

Solve.

14. Ben's model car traveled 345 feet. Sasha's model car traveled 410 feet. Whose car traveled farther?

______________ car traveled farther.

Draw or write to explain.

Use with text pages 593–596.

Name ____________________ Date ____________

Practice 20.8

Thousands, Hundreds, Tens, and Ones

Look at the blocks.
Write how many. Write the number.

1. 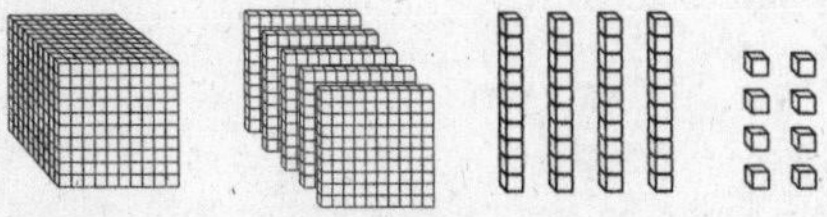

Thousands	Hundreds	Tens	Ones
1	5	4	8

1,548

2. 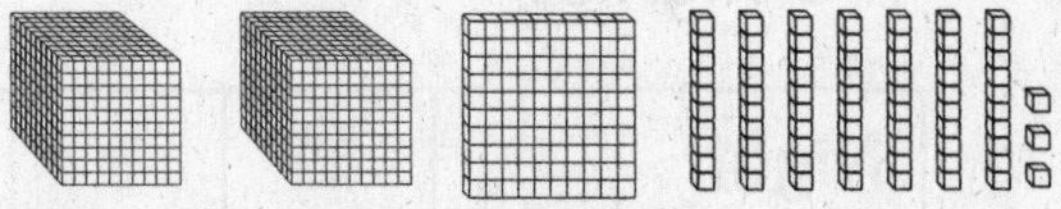

Thousands	Hundreds	Tens	Ones

____

3. 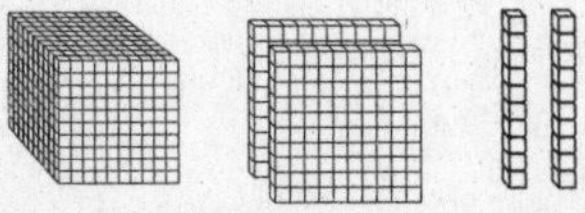

Thousands	Hundreds	Tens	Ones

____

4. 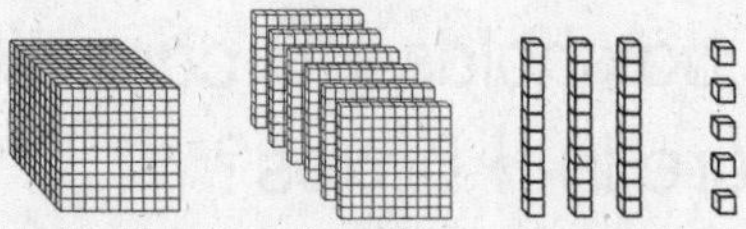

Thousands	Hundreds	Tens	Ones

____

5. 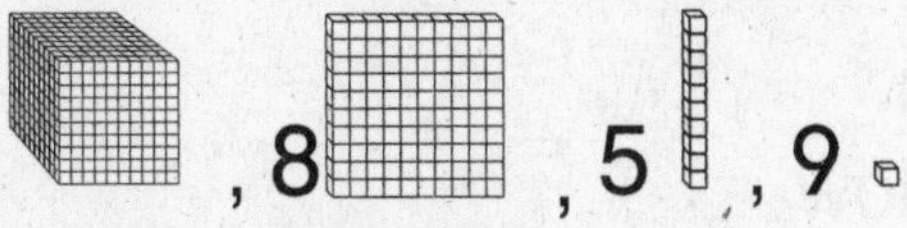

9 , 8 , 5 , 9

Thousands	Hundreds	Tens	Ones

____

6. 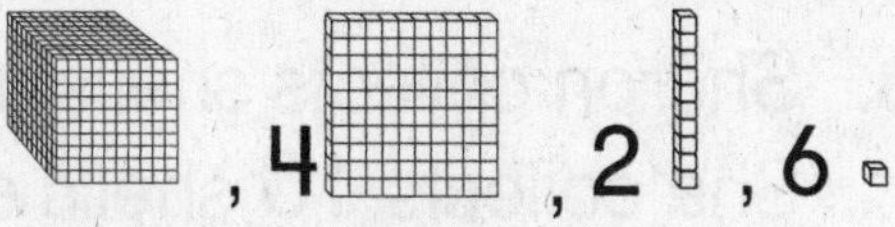

7 , 4 , 2 , 6

Thousands	Hundreds	Tens	Ones

____

Test Prep

Fill in the ○ for the correct answer.
NH means Not Here.

7. Which number does the model show?

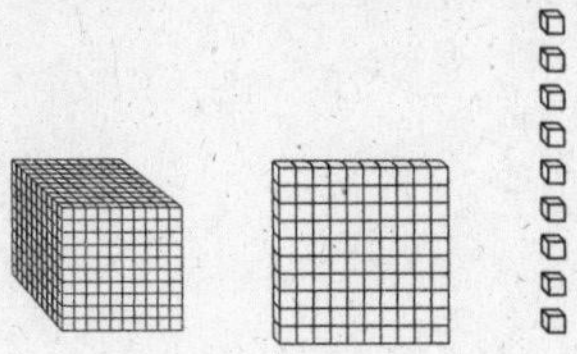

○ 1,019
○ 1,109
○ 1,190
○ NH

Use with text pages 597–599.

Name ______________________ Date ______________

Problem Solving: Make a Table

Make a table to solve.

1. Rachel knits 5 rows on her scarf each night. How many rows does she knit in 5 nights?

Night	1	2			
Rows	5	10			

Draw or write to explain.

_____ rows

2. Yusef keeps his toy cars in boxes. Each box holds 20 cars. How many cars are in 4 boxes?

Box	1			
Cars	20			

_____ cars

3. Sharon collects shells at the beach. She collects 10 shells each day. How many shells does she collect in 5 days?

Day					
Shells					

_____ shells

Test Prep

Fill in the ○ for the correct answer.

Draw or write to explain.

4. There are 30 muffins to put in boxes. Each box holds 6 muffins. How many boxes of muffins are there?

40	8	5	4
○	○	○	○

Use with text pages 601–603.

Name ______________________ Date ____________

Mental Math: Add Hundreds

Use the basic fact to help you add hundreds.

1. 8 + 1 = 9

8 hundreds + 1 hundred = 9 hundreds

800 + 100 = 900

2.

4	4 hundreds	400
+ 4	+ 4 hundreds	+ 400
	___ hundreds	

3.

7	7 hundreds	700
+ 2	+ 2 hundreds	+ 200
	___ hundreds	

4.

6	6 hundreds	600
+ 3	+ 3 hundreds	+ 300
	___ hundreds	

5.

1	1 hundred	100
+ 4	+ 4 hundreds	+ 400
	___ hundreds	

6.

2	2 hundreds	200
+ 6	+ 6 hundreds	+ 600
	___ hundreds	

7.

4	4 hundreds	400
+ 3	+ 3 hundreds	+ 300
	___ hundreds	

Test Prep

Fill in the ○ for the correct answer.
NH means Not Here.

8. On Monday, 400 people saw the play. On Tuesday, 500 people saw the play. Which addition sentence shows how many people saw the play in all?

○ 4 + 5 = 9 ○ 40 + 50 = 90 ○ 400 + 500 = 900 ○ NH

Use with text pages 611–612.

Name ______________________ Date ____________

Regroup Ones

Use Workmat 6 and place value blocks. Add.

1. $403 + 58 = $ 461	2. $128 + 417$	3. $324 + 247$	4. $543 + 126$
5. $817 + 143$	6. $339 + 156$	7. $145 + 7$	8. $426 + 235$
9. $603 + 278$	10. $754 + 28$	11. $405 + 404$	12. $464 + 127$
13. $453 + 119$	14. $227 + 146$	15. $218 + 367$	16. $785 + 208$

Test Prep

Solve.

Draw or write to explain.

17. Mindy has a collection of 342 shells. Ned gives her 39 shells. How many shells does she have in all?

_______ shells

Use with text pages 613–614.

Name ______________________ Date ______________

Regroup Tens

Use Workmat 6 and place value blocks. Add.

1. $\begin{array}{r} 187 \\ +\ 131 \\ \hline 318 \end{array}$	2. $\begin{array}{r} 123 \\ +\ 95 \\ \hline \end{array}$	3. $\begin{array}{r} 784 \\ +\ 42 \\ \hline \end{array}$	4. $\begin{array}{r} 261 \\ +\ 346 \\ \hline \end{array}$
5. $\begin{array}{r} 492 \\ +\ 331 \\ \hline \end{array}$	6. $\begin{array}{r} 196 \\ +\ 622 \\ \hline \end{array}$	7. $\begin{array}{r} 387 \\ +\ 130 \\ \hline \end{array}$	8. $\begin{array}{r} 661 \\ +\ 274 \\ \hline \end{array}$
9. $\begin{array}{r} 492 \\ +\ 157 \\ \hline \end{array}$	10. $\begin{array}{r} 381 \\ +\ 457 \\ \hline \end{array}$	11. $\begin{array}{r} 322 \\ +\ 182 \\ \hline \end{array}$	12. $\begin{array}{r} 194 \\ +\ 65 \\ \hline \end{array}$

Write the addends in vertical form.
Add.

13. 27 + 792 14. 184 + 161 15. 151 + 92 16. 494 + 465

Test Prep

Solve.

Draw or write to explain.

17. A farm truck travels 172 miles to the city. Then the truck drives back to the farm. How many miles does the truck travel in all?

_______ miles

Use with text pages 615–617.

Name ______________________ Date ______________

Practice 21.4

Add Money

Add.

1. $4.38 + 1.45 = $5.83

2. $1.75 + 3.50

3. $6.27 + 0.82

4. $1.92 + 7.63

5. $8.15 + 1.26

6. $4.78 + 2.61

7. $4.02 + 2.59

8. $5.12 + 3.91

Write the addends in vertical form.
Add.

9. $5.15 + $1.94

10. $1.90 + $1.99

11. $5.23 + $0.95

12. $5.65 + $3.25

13. $1.86 + $2.05

14. $2.75 + $0.30

Test Prep

Fill in the ○ for the correct answer.

15. Lauren earns money by walking dogs. One week, she earned $4.65. The next week, she earned $5.30. How much did Lauren earn for two weeks?

$10.95	$9.95	$5.35	$4.65
○	○	○	○

Use with text pages 619–620.

Name ______________________ Date ____________

Practice 21.5

Problem Solving: Guess and Check

Use guess and check to solve.

Remember
If the first guess is not the answer, try two other numbers.

Lunch Menu			
Sandwich	$1.25	Milk	$0.20
Slice of Pizza	$1.50	Smoothie	$0.70
Salad	$1.00		
Muffin	$1.75		

Draw or write to explain

1. José spent $2.25 for lunch. He got two items to eat. What did José buy?

sandwich and salad

2. George spent $1.70 for a drink and food. What two items did he buy?

____

3. Patricia spends $1.40 for two drinks. What does she buy?

____

Test Prep

Fill in the ○ for the correct answer. NH means Not Here.

4. Anne spent $1.90. What did she buy?

muffin and milk	sandwich and smoothie	slice of pizza and milk	NH
○	○	○	○

Mental Math: Subtract Hundreds

Use the basic fact to help you subtract hundreds.

1. 6 − 3 = ___3___

 6 hundreds − 3 hundreds = ___3___ hundreds

 600 − 300 = ___300___

2. 4 4 hundreds 400
 − 1 − 1 hundreds − 100

 hundreds

3. 8 8 hundreds 800
 − 2 − 2 hundreds − 200

 hundreds

4. 7 7 hundreds 700
 − 2 − 2 hundreds − 200

 hundreds

5. 9 9 hundreds 900
 − 8 − 8 hundreds − 800

 hundred

6. 5 5 hundreds 500
 − 2 − 2 hundreds − 200

 hundreds

7. 7 7 hundreds 700
 − 3 − 3 hundreds − 300

 hundreds

Test Prep

8. The soup factory packs 500 cans on Tuesday and 300 cans on Wednesday. How many more cans does the factory pack on Tuesday?

Draw or write to explain.

_____ cans

Use with text pages 631–632.

Name ______________________ Date ______________

Practice 22.2

Regroup Tens

Use Workmat 6 and place value blocks. Subtract.

1.

H	T	O
	6	10
3	7	0
− 3	3	2
	3	8

2.

H	T	O
7	6	0
− 3	2	8

3.

H	T	O
1	8	3
−	4	5

4.

H	T	O
6	8	1
− 4	1	3

5.

H	T	O
8	5	2
− 4	0	7

6.

H	T	O
3	7	5
− 1	2	9

7.

H	T	O
4	7	5
− 4	1	6

8.

H	T	O
5	2	7
− 1	0	9

9.

H	T	O
4	2	5
− 1	1	6

Test Prep

10. There are 254 third graders at Brown School. There are 229 second graders. How many more third graders than second graders are there?

Draw or write to explain.

______ more third graders

Use with text pages 633–634.

Name ______________________ Date ____________

Practice 22.3

Regroup Hundreds

Use Workmat 6 and place value blocks. Subtract.

1. $\begin{array}{r} \overset{5}{\cancel{6}}\overset{14}{\cancel{4}}5 \\ -\ 282 \\ \hline 363 \end{array}$	2. $\begin{array}{r} 927 \\ -\ 751 \\ \hline \end{array}$	3. $\begin{array}{r} 816 \\ -\ 273 \\ \hline \end{array}$	4. $\begin{array}{r} 318 \\ -\ 155 \\ \hline \end{array}$
5. $\begin{array}{r} 829 \\ -\ 562 \\ \hline \end{array}$	6. $\begin{array}{r} 417 \\ -\ 162 \\ \hline \end{array}$	7. $\begin{array}{r} 947 \\ -\ 54 \\ \hline \end{array}$	8. $\begin{array}{r} 708 \\ -\ 355 \\ \hline \end{array}$
9. $\begin{array}{r} 619 \\ -\ 278 \\ \hline \end{array}$	10. $\begin{array}{r} 634 \\ -\ 82 \\ \hline \end{array}$	11. $\begin{array}{r} 273 \\ -\ 116 \\ \hline \end{array}$	12. $\begin{array}{r} 758 \\ -\ 494 \\ \hline \end{array}$
13. $\begin{array}{r} 673 \\ -\ 391 \\ \hline \end{array}$	14. $\begin{array}{r} 525 \\ -\ 482 \\ \hline \end{array}$	15. $\begin{array}{r} 748 \\ -\ 563 \\ \hline \end{array}$	16. $\begin{array}{r} 802 \\ -\ 450 \\ \hline \end{array}$

Test Prep

17. Mary has 342 coins in her collection. Lee has 291 coins. How many more coins does Mary have than Lee?

Draw or write to explain.

________ more coins

Name ______________________ Date ____________

Practice 22.4

Check Subtraction

Subtract.
Check by adding.

1.
```
   8 16
   3 9 6           238
 - 1 5 8         + 158
   2 3 8           396
```

2.
```
   5 6 8
 - 2 7 6         +
```

3.
```
   5 1 6
 - 4 7 5         +
```

4.
```
   8 2 6
 - 4 9 2         +
```

5.
```
   4 2 8
 - 2 8 3         +
```

6.
```
   8 5 2
 - 5 0 3         +
```

Test Prep

Fill in the ○ for the correct answer.

7. Use these digits: 1, 2, 3, 4, 5.
Make the greatest possible sum.
Use each digit only once.

542 + 31	534 + 21	543 + 21	534 + 12
○	○	○	○

Use with text pages 639–640.

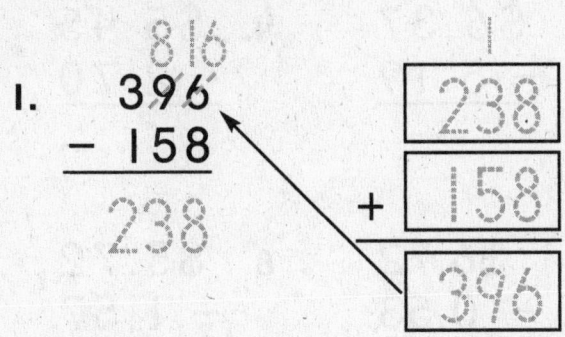

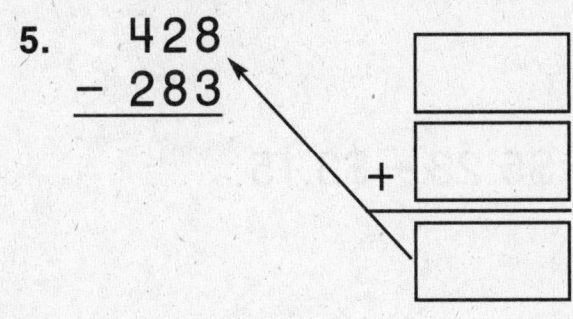

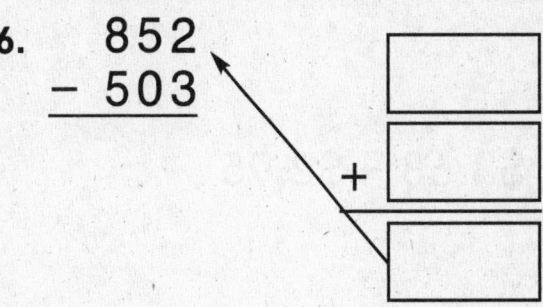

Subtract Money

Subtract.

2 15

1. $\begin{array}{r} \$3.55 \\ -\ 1.70 \\ \hline \$1.85 \end{array}$

2. $\begin{array}{r} \$5.72 \\ -\ \ .31 \\ \hline \end{array}$

3. $\begin{array}{r} \$6.37 \\ -\ 5.19 \\ \hline \end{array}$

4. $\begin{array}{r} \$5.45 \\ -\ 2.70 \\ \hline \end{array}$

5. $\begin{array}{r} \$8.93 \\ -\ 2.61 \\ \hline \end{array}$

6. $\begin{array}{r} \$9.50 \\ -\ 0.45 \\ \hline \end{array}$

7. $\begin{array}{r} \$6.72 \\ -\ 0.53 \\ \hline \end{array}$

8. $\begin{array}{r} \$5.72 \\ -\ 1.57 \\ \hline \end{array}$

Write the subtraction in vertical form.
Subtract.

9. $7.02 − $0.81

10. $1.98 − $0.39

11. $3.68 − $2.95

12. $5.23 − $3.15

Test Prep

Solve.

13. A pasta dinner costs $5.98.
A salad costs $1.59. How
much more does the pasta
dinner cost than the salad?

Draw or write to explain.

_____ more

Use with text pages 641–642.

Name ______________________ Date ______________

Practice 22.6

Problem Solving: Choose the Operation

Choose the operation. Write + or −. Then solve.

	Draw or write to explain
1. Lee's family drives to Dallas. They drove 342 miles on the first day and 261 miles on the second day. How many more miles did they drive on the first day?	342 ◯ 261 = _____ miles
2. Kim hiked 250 miles last year. She hiked 183 miles this year. How many miles did Kim hike in all?	250 ◯ 183 = _____ miles
3. Martin collected 147 shells at the beach. Sara collected 252 shells. How many more shells did Sara collect?	252 ◯ 147 = _____ shells

Test Prep

Fill in the ○ for the correct answer.

4. Which number sentence tells how many miles it is from Mountain Village to River Town?

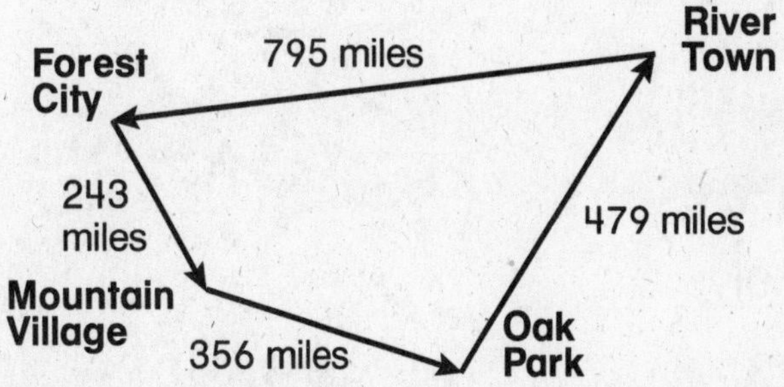

○ 479 + 243 = 722 ○ 356 − 243 = 113

○ 479 + 356 = 835 ○ 795 − 479 = 316